The Translation Debate

What Makes a Bible Translation Good?

Eugene H. Glassman

InterVarsity Press
Downers Grove
Illinois 60515

InterVarsity Press is the book-publishing division of Inter-Varsity Christian Fellowship, a student movement active on campus at hundreds of universities, colleges and schools of nursing. For information about local and regional activities, write IVCF, 233 Langdon St., Madison, WI 53703.

Distributed in Canada through InterVarsity Press, 1875 Leslie St., Unit 10, Don Mills, Ontario M3B 2M5, Canada.

Acknowledgment is made for permission to reprint from the following copyrighted material:
From Translating the Word of God by John Beekman and John Callow. Copyright © 1974 by the Zondervan Corporation. Used by permission.
From The Theory and Practice of Translation by Eugene A. Nida and Charles R. Taber. Used by permission from the United Bible Societies.
From Towards a Science of Translating by Eugene A. Nida. Used by permission from E. J. Brill publishers.

ISBN 0-87784-467-4

Printed in the United States of America

Library of Congress Cataloging in Publication Data

Glassman, Eugene H
    The translation debate.

    Includes bibliographical references and index.
    1. Bible—Translating.   2. Bible—Versions.   I. Title.
BS449.G5   220.5   80-29286
ISBN 0-87784-467-4

17	16	15	14	13	12	11	10	9	8	7	6	5	4	3	2	1
95	94	93	92	91	90	89	88	87	86	85	84	83	82	81		

I wish to express particular appreciation to

John A. Gration, *coordinator, Cross-Cultural Ministries, Department of Communications, Wheaton College Graduate School, who served as my adviser in the preparation of this project and to whom I am grateful for insightful questions which contributed substantially to its final form;*

and to

Eugene A. Nida, *translations secretary of the American Bible Society, and translations research coordinator for the United Bible Societies, an authority whose writings on translation are liberally quoted or referred to in this work, and who by making many helpful suggestions and clarifications graciously added to the net result of my efforts.*

To both Dr. Gration and Dr. Nida I acknowledge my indebtedness and offer my sincere thanks, while at the same time absolving them of any responsibility for imperfections remaining in the presentation of my material.

Abbreviations

ABS	American Bible Society
ASV	American Standard Version, 1901
BFBS	British and Foreign Bible Society
CBW	Charles B. Williams's translation
IDB	*Interpreter's Dictionary of the Bible*
JB	Jerusalem Bible
JBP	J. B. Phillips's translation
KJV	King James Version, 1611
LB	The Living Bible
LXX	Septuagint (the Old Testament in Greek)
NASB	New American Standard Bible
NEB	New English Bible
NIV	New International Version
NYT	*New York Times*
OED	Oxford English Dictionary
RSV	Revised Standard Version
RV	Revised Version, English, 1881, 1885
SIL	Summer Institute of Linguistics
TBT	*The Bible Translator*
TEV	Today's English Version (= Good News Bible)
UBS	United Bible Societies
WB	William Barclay's translation
WBT	Wycliffe Bible Translators

CHAPTER 1

TRANSLATION, THE THANKLESS TASK

T HE WORK OF TRANSLATION, whether of literature in general or of the Bible in particular, has traditionally and consistently been maligned. Even the titles of articles and books on the subject reveal doubts about translation as a legitimate area of human endeavor. For example:

"The Way of the Translator is Hard"[1]

The Trials of a Translator[2]

"Translation or Paraphrase"[3]

"The Precarious Profession"[4]

"Translation—The Art of Failure"[5]

"The Trouble with Translation"[6]

"The Polite Lie"[7]

"The Hazardous Art of Mistranslation"[8]

"The Torments of Translation"[9]

"Translation as Parody"[10]

"Traduttore, traditore"[11] (an Italian cliché meaning "Translators? Traitors!")

"If This be Treason: Translation and its Possibilities"[12]

In short, practically no translation of significance has ever seen the light of day without incurring the displeasure of many detractors. In this book I plan to deal with the broader issue only as it relates to Bible translation for several reasons. For one, that aspect is extremely relevant today. Constantly faced with new translations of the Bible, we must choose which ones we will use and for what purpose.

Second, having been engaged in Bible translation work since 1974, I have a keen interest in the matter.

Finally, translation as a science probably owes more to those who have sought to translate the Bible than to any other group of translators. Eugene Nida sums it up neatly:

> In terms of the length of tradition, volume of work, and variety of problems, Bible translating is distinctive. Beginning with the translation of the Hebrew Old Testament into Greek in the second and third centuries B.C., and continuing down to the present time... the major part of the Christian Scriptures [now] exist in the languages of at least 95 per cent of the world's population. Moreover, most of this work has been accomplished in relatively recent times. By the time of the invention of printing, approximately 500 years ago, only 33 languages had anything of the Bible, and even by the beginning of the nineteenth century only 71 languages possessed anything of the Scriptures. However, within the nineteenth century more than 400 languages received something of the Scriptures, and during the first half of the twentieth century some part of the Bible was translated into approximately 500 more languages and dialects.[13]

By the end of 1979 the total number of languages into which some portion of the Bible had been translated came to nearly 1,700.

Antipathy

As long ago as the fourth century A.D., Jerome, who translated the Bible into Latin (after first doing a number of the classics), wrote: "So great is the force of established usage that even acknowledged corruptions please the greater part, for they prefer to have their copies pretty rather than accurate."[14]

Earlier, he had complained rhetorically, "Is there a man, learned or unlearned, who will not, when he takes the volume into his hands, and perceives that what he reads does not suit his settled tastes, break out immediately into violent language, and call me a forger and a profane person for having the audacity to add anything to the ancient books, or to make any changes or corrections therein?"[15]

Jerome even referred to some of his critics as "two-legged asses"[16] and despaired of trying to explain anything to them. Quoting a Greek proverb he said, "It is idle to play the lyre for an ass."[17]

In the late fourteenth century A.D., John Wycliffe translated into English Jerome's Latin Bible (called the Vulgate). It was a period in history when Scriptures in the English language were regarded as dangerous heresy. One of Wycliffe's enemies, Henry Knyghton, deplored the fact that

> the gospel, which Christ delivered to the clergy and doctors of the church, that they might, themselves, sweetly administer to the laity and to weaker persons with the hunger of their mind according to the exigency of the times and the need of persons, did this Master John Wyclif translate out of Latin into English ... whence through him it became vulgar and more open to the laity, and [to] women who could read, than it used to be to the most learned of the clergy, even to those of them who had the best understanding.[18]

Although Wycliffe died a natural death in A.D. 1384, his remains, by order of the church, were dug up and burned forty-three years later. What Knyghton failed to recognize is that Wycliffe, by making the Scriptures "vulgar" (not as we use the term today but in the sense that it was used at that time, meaning colloquial, common or everyday), was only doing for his generation what Jerome had done for his. The related word *Vulgate* also means common or general.

In similar fashion William Tyndale felt the wrath of bigots of his time. They were convinced that the Bible should not be translated into English at all and that people should be satisfied with the Hebrew, Greek *and Latin!* Of them Tyndale remarked: "They will say it cannot be translated into our tongue, it is so rude. It is not so rude as they are false liars. For the Greek tongue agreeth more with the English than with the Latin. And the properties of the Hebrew tongue agreeth a thousand times more with the English than with the Latin."[19]

Then, in the course of an argument with a certain learned theologian, Tyndale exploded: "If God spare me life, ere many years, I will cause the boy that driveth the plough, to know more of the Scriptures than you do."[20]

Although his translation of the New Testament and much of the Old Testament later influenced the King James Version (KJV)—in fact, more than any other version did—Tyndale himself was kidnaped and tried for heresy in 1536, strangled at the stake and his body burned. All of that for merely daring to put the words of the Bible into common English.

Etienne Dolet was a French humanist who not only translated the classics but also published in A.D. 1540 "a brief but unsurpassed statement of translation principles."[21] Dolet likewise was accused of heresy for having "mistranslated" one of Plato's dialogs in a way that suggested a disbelief in immortality. At his trial in 1546 Dolet, then thirty-seven, was condemned as a confirmed atheist. He was tortured and strangled, and his body was burned along with copies of his books.

Moreover, even the King James Bible of A.D. 1611, that monument of dignity and reverence, has not always been as beloved as some people would like to think. Before

it appeared it was sharply criticized, many questioning
what need there was for it. In fact, it was so objectionable
to many people of its time that they would have nothing
to do with it. The Pilgrims, for example, would not even
allow it on board the *Mayflower,* preferring instead the
Geneva Bible of 1560 (which was also the Bible of William
Shakespeare). For at least forty years the new Bible had to
fight for its position. Indeed, the translators of the KJV in
their dedication to His Majesty more than once anticipated
the criticism of their work with the use of such expressions
as "censures," "calumniations," "hard interpretations,"
"malign" and "maligned," "bitter censures" and "unchari-
table imputations." They had expected to be reviled, and
their expectations were fulfilled.

This kind of attitude has persisted into modern times.
For example, considerable ire over the translation of
certain passages was stirred up after publication in 1952 of
the complete Revised Standard Version (RSV) of the Bible
—the New Testament of which had come out in 1946, with
similar disfavor. Some Christian ministers became so in-
censed that they publicly burned pages or copies of the RSV
Bible. In that connection someone observed that we have
made at least some progress since the Middle Ages: nowadays we burn only the translation—in the old days they
burned the translator.

The Living Bible (LB), a paraphrase which has become a
publication phenomenon of our day, was originally rejected by four publishers. That forced its author, Kenneth
Taylor, to have its first portions privately printed in 1962
on credit in a limited edition of 2,000 copies.[22]

Finally, publication of the *Good News Bible* (New Testament in 1966, full Bible in 1976) illustrates once again that
in matters of religious terminology people are very, very
slow to change, feeling that any alteration in the words of
the Bible as they have learned them is tantamount to heresy.
Nida explains: "They do not realize that what is really
changing is their own language and that, in order to pre-

serve the meaning of the original message, the form of language must be altered from time to time so as to adjust the content of the message to the constantly changing forms of expression."[23]

Thus reaction to Today's English Version (TEV, as the *Good News Bible* is also called) runs the gamut from surprised approval ("This can't be the Bible; I can understand it!") to vitriolic disdain ("This Bible is a masterpiece of Satan!").

Pedantry

Translation work has not only been hindered by antipathy, but also by literary pedantry. Such snobbery appears in various forms, from the pride that certain people take in their ability to read another language to the pride that insists that "a book is not read well unless it is read in its native tongue" and that "only then is it read at all."[24]

In an article entitled "How to Choose a Bible" Gerald Hawthorne pokes tongue-in-cheek fun at that kind of scholarly purist: "There is no substitute for knowing the Bible from the languages in which it was originally written. Hence my ultimate recommendation is that the Bible reader learn Hebrew and Greek! But this is not a likely possibility for most readers. Alternatively, pause a moment to give thanks for the many English translations at your fingertips. Then suit the translation to the need."[25]

Admittedly, "translations are not the same thing as their originals,"[26] and may at times differ from their originals in content. Yet should readers be constantly reminded that "translations into other languages are impossible"[27] or that "nothing worth translating can be translated"?[28]

Certainly not, for as Nida insists, "There is nothing which can be said in one language which cannot be said in another unless the form in which the utterance occurs is a part of what carries the meaning"[29] (for example, in plays on words).

Nida further notes that

although it is possible to say in one language anything which can be said in another, one must not conclude that it is always possible in translating to carry over the entire meaning of an original text. In fact, the higher the literary quality of the source language text, the more difficult it is to do justice to it in translation. For the more a source text reflects the essential genius of the language it uses, the more difficult it is to reproduce an equivalent communication in any receptor language. Translation always involves certain loss of impact, particularly when an original text is of high literary merit. Nevertheless, the essential denotative content can be communicated, and some of the loss in connotation may be compensated for by equivalent, though different, devices in the receptor language.[30]

Others complain of the sad state of the art of translating—and that seldom do artists of language do the translating of a work. They may recall the lament of John Denham in the seventeenth century:

Such is our pride, our folly and our fate,
That only those who cannot write, translate . . .[31]

Robert Pick, however, writing on the problem of translation as "literature's greatest challenge," describes as intellectual snobs those people who insist that "no one can possibly understand a book fully and appreciate its beauty unless he is able to read its original."[32] Pick adds, "Great translations, . . . not their originals, become part of the literature of their own language." The King James Version of the Bible is a good example.

One gets the feeling that some scholars, having worked so hard to acquire Greek or some other foreign tongue, proudly imagine that the "fellow down there with his translation" (sometimes called a "pony") surely can't get much out of it.[33] Such scholars resemble wealthy persons who, resentful that the poor should enjoy at a cheap price what they have spent so much for, are led to deny even the possibility of inexpensive entertainment. "Thus the snooty fisherman with the $100 outfit can't see why trout should let themselves be caught by the kid with home-made pole and line."[34]

Granted that masterpieces of translation are rare and that even those gain acceptance only with the passage of time, their rarity should not force us to conclude that the effort should not have been made at all. As Bandini points out, half a loaf—and if by good translation we can have nine-tenths of a loaf, all the better—is preferable to no loaf at all.[35] Most people simply would not have access to classical literature, much less Holy Scripture, were it not for translations. Even scholars who can read Greek and Latin classics in the original and who disparage reading them in translation are inclined to forget that they themselves are probably helpless before Sanskrit, Arabic or Chinese classics. Not all worthwhile literature has been written in Latin, Greek or Hebrew!

Confusion

A more serious problem than either antipathy or pedantry is the confusion in people's minds as to what constitutes a good translation and how it can be distinguished from a bad one. *The Bible Translator* (TBT), a quarterly begun in 1950 "for the assistance of Bible translators," called attention to such confusion in poignant words:

> There is a tendency among Bible translators and the Christian public in general to regard *translation* as always good and *paraphrase* as inevitably bad. So often one hears the comment, "But that is only a paraphrase," or "Why doesn't he translate instead of paraphrase?" To describe some rendering as a paraphrase is almost inevitably a severe criticism. In fact, in some circles the only condemnation that one needs to pass on any new version of the Bible is to call it a paraphrase. On the other hand, a "translation" is generally regarded as quite proper, and to call it a "faithful translation" means for some persons that the work is more or less a literal rendering. Unfor-

tunately, in the minds of many people "faithful translation" describes the degree of conformity to the King James Version.[36]

With publication in the twentieth century alone of over seventy *English* versions of the Bible or some portion of it, the issue is still much alive. Some of them, like the *New American Standard Bible* (NASB), are translations in the more or less traditional sense. Some, like *The Living Bible* (LB), are admitted paraphrases. Others fall somewhere in between. Some—for example, J. B. Phillips's *The New Testament in Modern English* (JBP), *The Living Bible* (LB) and the *Good News Bible* (TEV)—have proven extremely popular. Others have scarcely even been heard of.[37]

Many people engaged in Bible translation work have come to distinguish two essential elements in a language: its form and its meaning. One of the components, *form,* is crucial to an understanding of good translation and, therefore, of good communication. Beekman and Callow note that

all translators are agreed that their task is to communicate the meaning of the original. There is no discussion on this point. There is discussion, however, concerning the linguistic form to be used. Some believe that the meaning of the original is best communicated by translating into a linguistic form which closely parallels that of the original language. Others believe that by translating into the natural form of the receptor language [that is, the language being translated into], whether this parallels the form of the original or not, the meaning of the original is best communicated.

The choice which the translator makes between these two approaches will determine whether his translation will be classed as literal or idiomatic. These two terms classify a translation in regard to its linguistic form; they do not classify a translation on the basis of the meaning that it communicates which, of course, in a faithful translation should always represent the literal meaning of the

original text. If its form corresponds more to the form of
the original text, it is classed as *literal;* if its form corresponds more to the form of the receptor language . . .
then it is classed as *idiomatic.* Even though there are few,
if any, translations that are completely literal or completely idiomatic, each has been produced with one or
the other approach in mind.[38]

Significantly, the word *paraphrase* is not applied to either
type of translation, since linguists do not use the word in
that sense. More will be said on this point in the following
chapter, but the fact is that many renderings of biblical text
in any version *are* paraphrases pure and simple. However,
calling them that does not make them any less correct. It
is regrettable that a false distinction between translation
and paraphrase has produced a prejudice, automatically
labeling translation as good and paraphrase as bad, without
even defining the terms.

As Nida points out, "For the most part such expressions
as literal vs. free, translation vs. paraphrase, and words vs.
sense are essentially battle cries for those who wish to de-
fend their own work or criticize the work of others."[39]

Those interested in Bible translation tend to line up at
one extreme or the other, depending on their theology or
lack of it. Evangelicals who hold a so-called high view of
Scripture often favor a close and literal rendering of the
text while others tend to be freer in their translating. But,
as Nida further cautions, "It would be quite wrong . . . to
assume that all those who emphasize fully meaningful
translations necessarily hold to a neo-orthodox (or even
unorthodox) view of inspiration; for those who have combined orthodox theology with deep evangelistic or missionary convictions have been equally concerned with the need
for making translations entirely meaningful."[40] As such
persons see it, if "faith comes by hearing, and hearing by
the word of God" (Rom. 10:17), then that Word must come
to people in a language they can understand—and not only
can understand, but will not *mis*understand.

David's words in Psalm 139:16, for example, are given in the KJV as: "Thine eyes did see my substance, yet being unperfect; and in thy book all my members were written, which in continuance were fashioned, when as yet there was none of them." Literal and word-for-word? Mostly, but hardly meaningful in English as it is used today; and therefore not justified by the mere expediency of calling it *translation*. On the other hand, the same text in the TEV reads: "You saw me before I was born. The days allotted to me had all been recorded in your book, before any of them ever began." Literal and word-for-word? No, but hardly to be rejected because it changes the *form* to convey the original *meaning,* that is, because it is a *paraphrase* in the linguistically correct sense of the word. For equally striking contrasts compare the renderings of 2 Corinthians 3:10 or 10:13-16 in the KJV or the American Standard Version (ASV) of 1901 with those in the newer versions.

Nida rightly contends that "there are legitimate and illegitimate paraphrases. The literal word-for-word translation cannot be justified purely by calling it a 'translation.' Nor must a paraphrase be rejected simply by contending that it is such. There are literal, blind translations, biased translations, and excessively free translations—all of which are to be rejected. Similarly, one must emphatically reject paraphrases which are made for the sake of novelty of expression or designed to satisfy the translator's private whim."[41]

Early in my investigation of this subject I tended to think of it as *the translation-paraphrase dilemma.* After more consideration of the word *dilemma,* however, I began to realize that the word generally stands for a choice between two equally undesirable alternatives. I abandoned it because I do not believe that translation and paraphrase are either undesirable or alternatives. Based on my study of the problem in linguistic work for a number of years and specifically in Bible translation, I would rather regard it as a *debate* in the nontechnical, informal sense of that word—since the issue refuses to go away. About translation and paraphrase I would also ask whether the question is one of either/or or rather one of both/and. I am convinced that the latter is the correct point of view.

In developing the subject I will first try to clarify some key terms involved: *translate, interpret* and *paraphrase.* Then I will look at some examples that the Bible gives us of itself as "translator." After that I will contrast the two major ways of translating the Bible and call attention to the contribution that crosscultural (that is, missionary) translations have made to the debate. Finally I will suggest some basic guidelines to control us in any translational situation, which, if followed, would resolve the translation debate.

Although for purposes of illustration I will cite references from many versions of the Bible, my aim in doing so is neither to approve unreservedly nor reject categorically any of the versions thus referred to.

CHAPTER 2

TRANSLATE, INTERPRET, PARAPHRASE

ANY STUDY OF TRANSLATION vis-à-vis paraphrase must take into account the usage of the terms *translate*, *interpret* and *paraphrase* (with, of course, their derivatives as nouns, adjectives and so on).

Translate
The word *translate* literally means "to bear or carry across." In the sense applicable to our subject, it means "to turn from one language into another, to change into another language, retaining the sense; to render; to express in other words; to paraphrase."[1]

The Oxford English Dictionary (OED) notes that the phrases given here represent "the chief current sense" and quotes Locke (1690) as using the word in its absolute sense: "This is to translate, and not to define, when we change two words of the same significance one for another."[2] The OED also gives an example from Shakespeare *(The Merry Wives of Windsor,* I. iii. 54) to show how the word occurs in a *figurative* sense. Thus, "He hath studied her will; and translated her will; out of honesty, into English." In short, the word in the sense in which we normally use it means to interpret, explain, express one thing in terms of another. The word in that sense does not occur in the English of the KJV at all.

Interpret
Basically, the word *interpret* comes from two components, "between" and "to spread abroad." Although the OED says that the word now means "to expound the meaning of, to render clear or explicit, to elucidate or to explain," it does note that the word formerly also meant "to translate" but that such usage is now obsolete.[3] In modern English, to *interpret* usually refers to an immediate *oral* translation of a message. For written texts, we generally use the word *translate* to indicate a more or less literal rendering and *interpret* to indicate a translation plus commentary on the translation.

The word *interpret* appears in our English Bible in a variety of contexts:

(a) Instantaneous, oral translation from one language into another. For example, "And they knew not that Joseph understood them; for he spake unto them by an interpreter" (Gen. 42:23 KJV).

(b) Literal, verbal translation, or "meaning," much as one finds in a dictionary. Matthew 1:23; Mark 5:41; John 1:38, 42; 9:7; Acts 9:36 and Hebrews 7:2 are examples of this sense, rendered by the KJV as "which being interpreted is," "which by interpretation is called," "which is by interpretation" and so on, but by most modern versions with the words "which means," "this means" or simply "meaning." We will look at that usage in Scripture in more detail in chapter three.

Other uses of the word *interpret* in Scripture are not

important for our purposes, but for the sake of complete-
ness they can be cited as (c) applying to dreams (Gen. 40
and 41), (d) in the sense of exposition (as Lk. 24:27; Dan.
7—12; Job 33:23 and 2 Pet. 1:20), and (e) referring to unknown "tongues" (1 Cor. 12:10; 14:5, 13-15, 27-28).

In any case, the activity of translating or interpreting
is ancient, dating at least as far back as Babylon's Ham-
murabi (almost two thousand years before Christ, though
the precise date is uncertain). We know that a considerable
part of Babylon's official business was carried on by corps
of scribes who translated royal edicts into the various
languages of the empire.

Esther 8:7-9 (TEV) gives a classic example of that sort of
activity in the Medo-Persian Empire under King Ahasuerus
(Xerxes) in the fifth century B.C. (although neither the
word *translate* nor the word *interpret* occurs in the passage):

King Xerxes then said to Queen Esther and Mordecai,
the Jew, "Look, I have hanged Haman for his plot against
the Jews, and I have given Esther his property. But a
proclamation issued in the king's name and stamped
with the royal seal cannot be revoked. You may, however, write to the Jews whatever you like; and you may
write it in my name and stamp it with the royal seal."

This happened on the twenty-third day of the third
month, the month of Sivan. Mordecai called the king's
secretaries and dictated letters to the Jews and to the gov-
ernors, administrators, and officials of all the 127 prov-
inces from India to Sudan. The letters were written to
each province in its own language and system of writing
and to the Jews in their language and system of writing.

Inherent in the definitions of both *translate* and *interpret,*
of course, is the concept that regardless of the *form* used,
what is carried across from one language to another is
the *meaning* of the original writer or speaker. If that
meaning is lost—whether by addition, omission or distortion—then neither translation nor interpretation takes
place.

Paraphrase

We are confronted with a greater problem when we come to the third key word. *Paraphrase* is made up of two elements, "beside" or "alongside of" and "to declare" or "tell." Its first and primary meaning is *to tell or say the same thing in other words.* Absolutely essential to that definition is the word *same.*

In time, however, the word also came to mean a fuller and clearer expression of the sense of a passage or text, and even a free rendering or amplification of a passage.[4] Such a "translation with latitude" ignores the concept of saying the *same* thing and offers scope for all sorts of interpretation and comment. Regrettably, it is this sense of the word *paraphrase* which most people understand today.

The first recorded use of the word in the English language is Udall's in A.D. 1548 in *The Paraphrase of Erasmus upon the Newe Testament:* "Thou hast here good Christian reader the paraphrase of Erasmus upon the ghospell. ... A paraphrase is a plain settyng foorth of a texte or sentence more at large."[5]

Interestingly, the Greek word from which *paraphrase* derives does not even occur in the New Testament or early Christian literature surveyed by Arndt and Gingrich in their *Lexicon,* although Liddell and Scott give seven examples of it from the classical literature. E. A. Sophocles' *Lexicon* shows that the word was used twice by Origen in the third century A.D. in the sense of perverting or misinterpreting the meaning of something.

In the minds of the average Bible reader today the word *paraphrase* commonly means a very free, loose and therefore inaccurate translation, in which the translator is subjective rather than objective, and puts his or her own ideas into the text, thus biasing the resultant translation. Bible translation specialists are hence reluctant to use the word at all. Beekman and Callow do not apply the term to the types of translation they discuss, saying that "when used to characterize a translation, it is generally with a pejorative sense meaning that an attempt has been made to render the text in a form that is clearer to us than it was to the original readers with the result that extraneous information and unnecessary interpretations are found."[6]

In other words, a translation which deviates from the meaning of the original writer or speaker is not a translation at all. But neither should it be called a paraphrase, for "the usage of the word 'paraphrase' in linguistic circles is not applied to translation but rather to two different statements *in a single language* which have the same meaning. One statement is called the paraphrase of the other. The counterpart of paraphrase within a language is translation between languages. That is, when we find two different statements with the same meaning and each is in a different language, one statement is a translation of the other."[7]

Nida and Taber also prefer to use the word *paraphrase* in its technical sense as found in linguistics and related disciplines. As such it is distinguished in three particular ways: "(1) it is intralingual rather than interlingual, i.e., it is 'another way of saying the same thing' in the *same* language; (2) it is rigorous, in that there are no changes in the semantic components: no additions, no deletions, no skewing of relationships, only a different marking of the same relations between the same elements; (3) specifically as it relates to back-transformation, it is aimed at restatement at a particular level, that of the kernels."[8]

To clarify those important insights let us look at a few examples. The first comes from Barclay Newman, who illustrates by supposing that the original text is: "John hit Bill on the nose."[9] It is quite possible without changing the meaning at all to render this statement in at least four other ways in English (because, remember, we are looking for other ways to say the same thing in the same language). Including the original, these are:

John hit Bill on the nose. (6 words)

Bill was hit by John on the nose. (8 words)
Bill was hit on the nose by John. (8 words)
Bill was hit on the nose. John did it. (9 words)
John hit Bill. He hit him on the nose. (9 words)

Although the last two sentences represent a 50 per cent increase in length over the original (all of the derived sentences consist of more words), they all say essentially the same thing. Emphasis and style may differ, but the meaning is unchanged. In the sense in which I will use the word *paraphrase*, these are all paraphrases or, if you will, "faithful renderings."

We could also have restated the original sentence (as Newman suggests) in other ways, as follows:

John hit Bill on the nose because he did not like Bill (12 words). Such a statement (because...) is a value judgment made by the translator or paraphraser, bringing in a suggestion not stated in the original. It is therefore neither a translation nor a paraphrase, since it changes the meaning by *addition*.

Bill was hit on the nose (6 words). Although this statement keeps the same number of words as the original, it leaves out important information, namely, that it was John who hit Bill. This, too, is neither a translation nor a paraphrase, since it changes the meaning by *deletion* or *omission*.

John hit Bill on the nose. Bad boys always behave that way (12 words). The information given here goes far beyond what was mentioned in the original, offering as it does the translator's or paraphraser's own point of view. It is therefore neither a translation nor a paraphrase because it is not faithful and it does not say the same thing. The translator or paraphraser here seems to be trying to "help out" the original writer or speaker by saying more than that person intended.

Nida and Taber's first two points concerning faithfulness in paraphrase are thus rather straightforward. But their third point about "back-transformation," "restatement" and "kernels" may need some clarification.

Two helpful examples are the expressions "the gospel of God" (Rom. 1:1) and "the gospel of Christ" (2 Cor. 10:14), which seem in their surface structure (that is outward, apparent form) to be the same. They may easily be misinterpreted (and already have been mistranslated). After comparing all relevant contexts in which these two expressions occur it can be reasonably inferred that "the gospel *of* God" means "the good news which *comes from* God" whereas "the gospel *of* Christ" means "the good news *about* Christ." The source of that good news is God but the substance or subject of it is Christ. The surface structure in both cases is *of* but the kernels are different, one meaning "comes from" and the other "about, with reference to, concerning."

It is at the level of basic structural elements (called "kernels"), out of which the more elaborate surface structures of a language are derived, that paraphrase is most essential. Within the same language, one analyzes the message and reduces its surface structure to its underlying kernels. Such a process is called back-transformation, which is highly important to the translator not only because such kernels exist in all languages but because "languages agree far more on the level of the kernels than on the level of the more elaborate structures."[10]

Nida is correct in suggesting that

some of our confusion comes from a purely quantitative perspective. We begin to think of translations in terms of the number of corresponding words. Such a mechanical view of things—straining at gnats and swallowing camels—is practically useless. It really should make no difference to us whether a translation of a term in Greek consists of one or five words; or whether, on the other hand, we render an entire phrase in Greek by a single word in an aboriginal language—a thing which often does occur. We are not concerned primarily with counting words and parts of words. Our objective must be in finding *the closest equivalence in meaning.* The insistence upon the principle of closest semantic equivalence actually renders obsolete the meaningless discussions which go on between the defenders of "translation" and the advocates of "paraphrase."[11]

Since genuine translation from one language into another is not a matter of matching phrases or sentences word for word, often with misleading or even absurd results, one is forced to agree with Nida that "the traditional arguments about 'translation' as legitimate and 'paraphrase' as forbidden are really quite beside the point. It is not a matter of how many words are necessary to reproduce the meaning of the original, but *the degree of fidelity* with which the thought of the original is expressed in another language. It is not infrequent that a so-called paraphrase is far closer to the meaning of the original than a more tight-laced translation."[12]

For this reason F. F. Bruce objects to the casual criticism of J. B. Phillips's version of the New Testament by some who call it "a paraphrase rather than a translation" (though Phillips himself in his new revised edition, 1972, does not use the word *paraphrase* with reference to his text).[13] As Bruce points out, it is easy to spout such terms without defining them; and it is seldom easy for the layperson to tell where translation ends and paraphrase (in its broader sense of interpretation) begins. Bruce suggests that what Phillips gives is "a meaning-for-meaning translation. And what is the purpose of a translation if it does not communicate the meaning?"[14] Of course, one must be careful to underline the word *the;* it is not just *any* meaning which we want from the text but *the* meaning which the author intended.

Clearly Phillips has produced one of the most readable and meaningful versions of the New Testament in present-day English. Further, there is no denying that "time and time again *The Living New Testament* [LB, an acknowledged paraphrase] is a faithful, clear, idiomatic and expressive representation of the meaning of the original."[15]

Yet, Phillips renders Luke 13:11 as "In the congregation was a woman who for eighteen years had been ill from some psychological cause . . . " and LB translates 2 Timothy 3:16 as "The whole Bible [all sixty-six books, some of which had not even been written at that point in history] was given to us by inspiration from God." These particular renderings must be rejected on the ground that they are not legitimate paraphrase (in the sense of having been restructured on the level of the sentence kernels). Rather, they provide new information not intended by the original authors.

The question is not whether one happens to be in agreement with the underlying philosophical or theological reasons for the renderings. It is whether such translations are really saying the *same* thing as the original (that is, are paraphrased on the level of the kernel structures), or are saying something different (that is, paraphrased on the level of surface structure, with additions, deletions or skewing of the original meaning).

In *The Trials of a Translator,* Ronald Knox cautioned translators against being frightened by the word *paraphrase.* Such fear, he says,

> is a bogey of the half-educated. As I have already tried to point out, it is almost impossible to translate a sentence without paraphrasing. . . . When St. Paul describes people as "wise according to the flesh" [1 Cor. 1:26], the translator is under an obligation to paraphrase. In English speech, you might be called fat according to the flesh, or thin according to the flesh, but not wise or foolish. The flesh here means natural, human standards of judging, and the translator has got to say so. "Wise according to the flesh" is Hebrew in English dress; it is not English.[16]

It should be remembered that emphasis on meaningful

translation is not some latter-day perversion dreamed up by twentieth-century heretics. As long ago as the fourth century A.D., Jerome frankly admitted that he translated "sense for sense and not word for word."[17] In support he called attention to the manner in which the New Testament writers freely quoted or adapted the original Hebrew or Septuagint (LXX) in their own writings. There was certainly no slavish literalism there!

Likewise, Martin Luther, in his translation of the German Bible, is an outstanding example of one who strove for complete meaningfulness and full intelligibility. He defended his principles of translation, citing a number of points that many today would call paraphrase. The difficulty we find in Luther's German today does not reflect badly on its quality for the age in which it was translated. It is evidence only that languages are constantly changing and, therefore, that translations of the Scriptures also need to be brought up to date. In fact, it is reckoned that "no Scripture is regarded as fully effective for more than fifty years, so rapid is the change which takes place in languages."[18]

One of Luther's contemporaries, Etienne Dolet of France (mentioned in chapter one), deserves credit for the first formulation of "fundamental principles of translation." Nida summarizes them as follows:

1. The translator must understand perfectly the content and intention of the author whom he is translating.

2. The translator should have a perfect knowledge of the language from which he is translating and an equally excellent knowledge of the language into which he is translating.

3. The translator should avoid the tendency to translate word for word, for to do so is to destroy the meaning of the original and to ruin the beauty of the expression.

4. The translator should employ the forms of speech in common usage.

5. Through his choice and order of words the translator should produce a total overall effect with appropriate "tone."[19]

Coming as they do from the year 1540, these principles sound remarkably up to date.

In 1680 John Dryden took the formulation of principles a step further by recognizing three basic kinds of translation: (1) metaphrase, or word-for-word and line-by-line rendering; (2) paraphrase, in which the author's work is kept in view but only the sense rather than words are followed; and (3) imitation, in which the translator takes the liberty of varying both the words and the sense and also leaving both if he or she feels "the spirit of the original" requires it.[20] Dryden personally favored the golden mean of *paraphrase,* noting with regard to metaphrase that "it is impossible to translate verbally and well at the same time."[21]

A friend once wrote to me: "In all this translation work I believe faithfulness to the Hebrew and Greek original is still more important than easy understandableness. What do you think? We still have the Holy Spirit to make God's meaning clear." I cannot agree with that sentiment, even though it is sincere and well intended. For one thing, it places the Bible on the level of a magical document or fetish, which, even if not understood, can and will do its work. For another, it assumes a measure of grace for all humanity in the working of the Holy Spirit that not even Christians themselves can always claim. "We" may "have the Holy Spirit to make God's meaning clear" but even "we" have trouble at times understanding the real meaning from the translations that have been handed down to us. How can we assume, then, that anyone of lesser interest and concern will make sense of it?

Take the phrase "the righteousness of God" in Romans 1:17 as an example. Most people tend to think that the righteousness spoken of there is an attribute of God, his own personal characteristic, rather than a provision of God based on the requirement of faith in Christ "from start to finish" (LB). Yet even though it has been pointed out that this passage must be restructured in order to communicate what the Greek actually means, many Bible translators are loath to make the clarification. In fact, as Nida comments,

> one committee refused [to clarify the Greek syntax in the language that they were working in] on the ground that if the laity could understand the Bible so readily, then what would the preachers have to do? However, a rendering which does not communicate the sense of the original is simply not a translation but a string of words, and any legitimate analysis of the adequacy of a translation must accept as a primary criterion of correctness the manner in which such a translation is understood by the majority of persons for whom it is designed.[22]

But such adequacy can be realized only by recognizing the legitimacy of paraphrase on the level of the kernels (as described above). A translator "must not be chained to any false ideas about inseparability between words and thoughts. *The relevant unit of meaning for the translator is not the word, but the message.*"[23] Note that *word* here is not capitalized, since it is used in a linguistic and not a theological sense.

Having pointed out that translation and paraphrase are two sides of the same coin, not to be pitted against each other at all, I will try to illustrate that point in the following chapter by looking at examples of "translation" as done by the Bible itself. We will see that even when the Bible itself "translates" it does so, not in a literal, slavishly word-for-word manner, but in a broader sense, concentrating on the meaning and intent of the passage.

CHAPTER 3

THE BIBLE AS TRANSLATOR

Pertinent to any discussion of translation and paraphrase is the question of how the Bible itself, when it has occasion to do so, translates.

Septuagint (LXX)
We need not go into the manner in which the Septuagint (LXX) reflects the original Hebrew text which it translates. Yet we should remember that the LXX is by far the oldest, most important and most influential translation of the Bible in any language. It is the Greek translation of the Hebrew Old Testament, prepared, as is generally conceded, during the third century B.C. It was done in Hellenistic Greek, not in the *koine* (that is, common) Greek of the New Testament—although there is some similarity between the two. Grant and Rowley point out that "in its syntax . . . it is strongly tinged with Hebraisms, which give

it a distinct character of its own. The general tendency of the LXX translators was to be very literal, and they repeatedly followed Hebrew usage (notably in the use of pronouns, prepositions, and participial constructions) to an extent which runs entirely counter to the genius of the Greek language."[1]

The subject is mentioned here because New Testament writers often quoted the LXX, Luke and the writer of Hebrews doing so frequently and Matthew doing so least of all. For generations it was "the Bible" of Greek-speaking Jews in many countries, just as the KJV has been for many generations "the Bible" for multitudes of English speakers. In spite of that the LXX often differs from the Hebrew texts of the Old Testament we have today. Since it, rather than the Hebrew, is quoted so commonly by New Testament writers, we must assume one or more of the following probabilities:

(1) When New Testament writers quoted the Old Testament, they often did so from memory and were not concerned with the exact verbal correspondence we look for in quotations today.

(2) They may have made their own translations, on the spot as it were, just as I have often observed bi- and trilingual national speakers *read* the Bible in one language (the national, official one) and then, in the course of preaching, *render* it into an unwritten vernacular, giving the sense in their own words, but not being particularly careful about a precise word-for-word translation.

(3) They may have translated Aramaic or Hebrew texts that we no longer have that differ from the Masoretic text now generally followed in Hebrew translations.

(4) The LXX could actually have preserved meanings of Hebrew words that were current at the time it was translated but which were later lost. We simply do not know.

(5) Finally, the differences we recognize today between the LXX and the Masoretic text may in many cases have been deliberately or unconsciously introduced by New Tes-

tament writers who were guided by the Holy Spirit as they wrote down that fuller revelation which was given to complete the canon of Scripture.

Since the issue is too complex to resolve here, I mention it merely to suggest that a very old tradition exists for translating somewhat "loosely," and that only in relatively modern times have we been concerned with exact quotation, giving chapter, verse or page.

Many people are unaware that the chapter and verse divisions we have in our Bibles today are from a relatively late date. Chapter divisions, for example, go back to the thirteenth century A.D. and verse divisions to the sixteenth. The first English edition to use chapter numbers was Wycliffe's version of 1382. Verse divisions in the Greek New Testament were introduced by Robert Stephanus of Paris in 1551. The Latin Vulgate edition of 1555 was the first entire Bible to use chapter and verse numbers; the first English New Testament to contain them was the Geneva Bible of 1560.

When one recognizes that in earliest times not everyone could afford to have a personal copy of the Scriptures (which had to be hand-copied, not printed on presses as today), it is not surprising that a certain amount of flexibility in giving references from the Old Testament in the New was tolerated, possibly even to be expected, in contrast with our own day and age. Note, for example, the phrase "somewhere in the Scriptures" in Hebrews 2:6 and 4:4 (TEV).

Aramaic and Hebrew into Greek
The text of the Bible as translated, gives us a number of significant renderings that also suggest a place for latitude in translation.

Aramaic, a close cognate but not a derivative of Hebrew, was the mother tongue of Jews in the later period of the Old Testament and in New Testament times. As shown in 2 Kings 18:26, it had been used as an international and diplomatic language in the Assyrian Empire (eighth and seventh centuries B.C.); under the Persian Empire (sixth and fifth centuries B.C.) it was the official language. Both the Old and New Testaments show traces of the language.

A familiar Aramaic statement occurs in the book of Daniel (5:25-28). The words in Aramaic constitute the famous "handwriting on the wall" which King Belshazzar saw but was unable even with the help of his wise men to understand. The words were probably common enough, but their significance was hidden until Daniel was called.

Some take the words "mene, mene, tekel, upharsin" (KJV) or "mene, mene, tekel, and parsin" (RSV) to be a series of weights or monetary units. The assumption is that the Aramaic script (like the Hebrew) was unvocalized (thus *mn', mn', tql, prs*) and that the puzzle lay in pronouncing the right vowels to make the sentence or phrase meaningful. On this reckoning they read: "a mina, a mina, a shekel and a half-shekel." By changing the vowels of the first "mene" to make it imperative (from the verb meaning "to number") it could then read: "Number a mina, a shekel, and a half-shekel" (plural, literally "halves"). If other vowels are also changed (that is, by being supplied mentally), the nouns can become verbs meaning "numbered, weighed and divided." The TEV gives the following rendering: "Number, number, weight, divisions."

In any case, the *u* in "upharsin" is the connecting word *and*, which is ignored in the KJV but shown in the RSV. It is instructive that Daniel applied the verbal (rather than nominal) sense to the king, who is said to have been "weighed on the scales and found to be too light" and whose "kingdom is divided up and given to the Medes and Persians" (TEV). No matter which version one consults, one finds a certain freedom of rendering here which is a far cry from the rigid literalism some would urge on biblical translators. At the very least, most renderings of this verse would have to be considered paraphrases.

Moving into the New Testament, we find the instructive

occasion when Jesus spoke to Jairus's young daughter the words *Talitha koum* (Mk. 5:41) which in Aramaic mean literally "Maiden, arise (get up)!" But Mark in recording the incident tells us that this "means" (is to be interpreted or translated as) "Little girl, *I tell you to* get up." The italicized words "I tell you to" are included in Mark's Greek, even though the Aramaic did not have them. (The NEB ignores them and simply gives, "Get up, my child," a rather free rendering.) Of course Mark's translation is perfectly natural and normal and does not change the sense of the original in the least. It is, however, a change in its style. For pedants and purists who like to count words, the original Aramaic consisted of two words; the translated Greek rendering (found in our text) consists of five.

Likewise, the word *Golgotha* (the place where Jesus was crucified), whether one takes it as Aramaic or Hebrew, means simply "skull." However, Matthew (27:33), Mark (15:22) and John (19:17) in their Greek translate it as "a place of a skull" or "skull's place." Only Luke follows the Aramaic or Hebrew literally and exactly (in 23:33) by saying that "when they came to the place called 'Skull,' there they crucified him." The KJV renders the word as "Calvary" in the passage in Luke—actually a Latin word found only here in our English Bible—but most modern versions translate it as "the Skull." Except in Luke, however, the translation into Greek represents a stylistic expansion, perfectly justifiable, to be sure, but not in keeping with the rigidity desired by those who use the word *paraphrase* in a derogatory sense.

A similar argument might be made for the translation of the Aramaic word *Gabbatha* in John 19:13, except that its meaning is still uncertain. Arndt and Gingrich cite C. C. Torrey's contention that the word is really Latin (*gabata* = *platter*), adapted to the Aramaic language because the stone pavement looked like a platter.[2] Whether that is so or not, the Greek word found in our New Testament as a translation means "paved with blocks of stone" or "stone pavement or mosaic."[3] The TEV gives the translation as "The Stone Pavement," actually more precise than the KJV which says, "the Pavement" (which might be made of various kinds of materials).

While hanging on the cross Jesus uttered in Aramaic those famous opening words of Psalm 22: "My God, my God, why hast thou forsaken me?" (KJV) recorded in Matthew 27:46 and Mark 15:34. At this point the LXX reads: "My God, my God, look thou upon me, why hast thou forsaken me?" The phrase "look thou upon me" is not found in the Hebrew text but was added by the LXX translators. But both Matthew and Mark prefer to ignore the Greek (LXX) translation of the psalm already available to them and offer their own slightly different but adequate literal renderings into Greek.

Jerome raised this very point with his critics: "Let my critics tell me why the Septuagint introduces here the words 'Look thou upon me'.... They will answer no doubt that *no harm is done to the sense* by the addition of a couple of words."[4] The difference was one of style, not of substance, which Jerome then turned to his own defense by asking why his detractors would not allow *him* the same freedom of rendering, especially when he translated not the LXX but the Hebrew.

Some Aramaic words used in the New Testament are not translated into Greek (for example, *mammon* and *raka);* others are done so loosely and freely. Thus *mammon* in both the KJV and the RSV is merely transliterated as "mammon," it being assumed that readers will know (but why should they?) that the word means "wealth, riches, property, money." A number of the newer translations (for example, LB, NEB, TEV) show it as "money."

The Aramaic *raka* occurs in a rather difficult context where Christ warns about anger (Mt. 5:21-22). Three degrees of anger are mentioned: (a) being angry with one's brother, (b) calling one's brother *raka* and (c) saying, "O fool." The second of these the RSV renders as "insults his brother"; the KJV does not translate it at all but merely transliterates. Again, why should anyone today know that the word *raka* probably means "fool, empty-head, numbskull"? The newer translations are therefore correct in giving an up-to-date rendering of the word. Thus, "good-for-nothing" (TEV); "brainless idiot" (William Barclay [WB]); "contemptuously . . . a fool" (JBP); "idiot" (LB); "insults" (RSV) and "abuses" (NEB).

The word *corban* is translated by Mark (7:11) as "gift," but it is a gift in a special sense, something consecrated or dedicated to God (so "given to God" RSV). It is actually the word *sacrifice* found in Arabic and a number of other related languages of the Middle East. So, while the KJV is not wrong to say, "It is Corban, that is to say, a gift," it is not nearly so clear as the TEV which renders, 'This is Corban' (which means, it belongs to God)."

Hebrew words also are adapted in translation. For example, *rabbi* is literally "my lord or master," but it is translated in John 1:38 and other places as "teacher."

Such adaptation may include a change in the order of words, as in the prophecy (Mt. 1:23) which speaks of *Emmanuel,* a Hebrew word (or combination of words) which according to Hebrew order says, literally, "with us God." The translators of the KJV and others since then have had no qualms about reversing the order to "God with us." In his translation work Jerome noted that in the Holy Scriptures "even the order of the words is a mystery."[5]

Melchizedek, whose name is made much of in Hebrews 7:2, is said to have been both "King of Righteousness" and also "King of Peace" (= *Sālem*). The word actually is a combination of *Melchi* (= my king) and *Sedeq* (thus, My king is Sedeq); but *Sedeq* is related to the word *(T)sādaq,* meaning "righteousness." And *Sālem,* though literally meaning "safe, at peace," is often identified with Jerusalem (see Ps. 76:2 and Ezra 5:15 for the Aramaic form of the word). Thus a considerable play on words is required to get out of Melchizedek's name the meanings indicated. This is not to criticize such freedom in translation, but only to note that biblical writers themselves resorted to it at times.

Inevitability of Paraphrase

To complete our discussion of the Bible itself as a translator, let us look at a few references in the English Bible, especially in the KJV (since it is still held in highest esteem by most of my generation of English speakers).

When the King James translators were assigned their task, which was basically that of "revision," one rule laid down to guide them was to use another kind of type (italics were settled on) to indicate certain words in their text. Those were words the translators supplied which had to be added to complete the sense even though they did not actually occur in the originals. Such a rule was no more than a concession to linguistic reality and to the impossibility of exchanging one language for another without some adjustment in *form* to communicate the meaning. All editions of the KJV up to the present century showed such adjustments in italics. Now, however, some later editions have tended to drop the italics and use only one style of type.

Matthew 1:23 provides an interesting illustration. The KJV translators made some adjustment (paraphrase?) and failed to make some others. For example, the Greek says "the virgin" (a particular one), while the KJV, RSV and some others say simply "a virgin." In this instance they chose to follow the Hebrew (of Is. 7:14) rather than the Greek of Matthew. Then the Greek idiom says "shall have in womb," which the translators gave as "shall be with child," a fair enough rendering for seventeenth-century English but hardly the literal translation that purists demand. The RSV, NEB and LB, with their "shall/will conceive," are clearly more up to date.

It is to the credit of the KJV committee, however, that they frequently *did* take the liberty to depart from word-for-word literalism and rephrase the text according to the demands of the receptor language. Regrettably, however, both here in Matthew 1:23 ("they shall call his name Emmanuel") and in 1:21 ("thou shalt call his name Jesus"), they settled for a literal rendering which, though it has become common (since this text is often used as a "memory verse"), is not English. Also regrettably, the NASB and the *New International Version: The New Testament* (NIV) do not improve on it but maintain the awkward literalness of the KJV, ASV and RSV. When a child is born into the home of an English speaker, we may "call" the child John or Bill, or "name" him John or Bill; but we *never* "call his name" John or Bill. To do so would evoke surprise or even puzzlement—unless, of course, our hearers, familiar with the KJV or one of these other versions of the Bible, thought we were trying to be "biblical."

In Mark 15:37, 39 and Luke 23:46 the KJV uses the rather archaic expression "gave up the ghost." This happens to be five words to render one Greek word, a practice certainly frowned on by those who believe in word-for-word correspondence in translation. The Greek word actually means "to breathe out" or "to expire"; the latter translation is found in Phillips in Mark 15:37 and Luke 23:46, in Charles B. Williams's translation (CBW) of the Mark passages and oddly enough seems to be supported even by Kubo and Specht.[6] Documents, terms and dates may "expire" in the 1980s, but *people* generally do not (at least, not in America). They simply "die," and there is nothing radical or inappropriate about saying so, as the TEV, NEB, Barclay and many other modern versions do.

Phillips (JBP) uses "died" in Mark 15:39, as does *The Jerusalem Bible* (JB). But the JB gives "breathed his last" in Mark 15:37 and Luke 23:46. "Breathed his last" is found in all three references of the RSV and in the Luke passage by Williams (CBW). The LB, in contrast, uses "died" in Luke but "dismissed his spirit" in Mark (both times). The latter phrase sounds more like *translationese* than English, since people simply do not "dismiss" spirits in the twentieth century.

A further example is seen in the translation of *mē genoito* in Luke 20:16; Romans 3:4, 6, 31; 6:2, 15; 7:7, 13; 9:14; 11:1, 11; 1 Corinthians 6:15; Galatians 2:17; 3:21 and 6:14. The phrase is consistently translated in the KJV as "God forbid," since it expresses a wish that something may not occur. But even a first-year student of Greek knows that *mē* does not mean "God" and *genoito* does not mean "forbid." Rather, *mē* is the negative and *genoito* is the optative form of the verb meaning "may/let it be." There is no objection to the KJV rendering, which acknowledges God as the one who permits or does not permit things to happen. It is pointed out only to show that here the translators definitely resorted to paraphrase and not to translation. Versions newer than the KJV use such expressions as "By no means!" "Never!" "Far from it!" "Certainly not!" "Not a bit of it!" and "God forbid" (Gal. 6:14 JBP). All of these are acceptable representations of the intent of the original text, the difference being one of style.

Hebrews 1:1 and 2 offer another interesting example. The Greek says merely that God "in these last days has spoken to us in son" (v. 2), words which to an English speaker's ear sound strangely incomplete. For that reason the KJV (and some other versions) have added the word "his" before "son," showing it in italics in some editions and omitting the italics in others. The point is that the Greek does not have the word *his* and that most translators (even those who did the KJV) have added it. This, too, is a form of paraphrase, an effort to say in a receptor language (in this case, English) what was said in the source language, even though the words do not match up one for one. With this rendering also there can be no objection since it is Jesus Christ who is clearly in view in the mind of the writer.

A subtle point, however, is generally overlooked in the translations, whether ancient or modern. The word *son* in verse 2 occurs without the article *the*. When the article *the* occurs in Greek, the word it is used with is certainly definite, indicating that something has been identified, either in the linguistic or nonlinguistic context of a communication. When the article does not occur (as here in Heb. 1:2), however, then the word it is omitted from may or may not be definite. Dana and Mantey point out that the lack of the article, especially in the predicate position, may be more qualifying than identifying.[7] It would seem that the contrast the writer of the letter to the Hebrews was making is that in former times God spoke off and on ("many times and in many ways") through the prophets, but in these last days spoke fully and finally through *such a one as a Son* (in contrast to one who was only a prophet). The former was a prophet-revelation, the latter a Son-revelation. It is impossible to bring this sense out in a literal word-for-word translation without resorting to paraphrase.

One more example will be given to show that at times a strict, literal, word-for-word translation is impossible and that to make any sense one has to paraphrase. That was as true for the King James translators as it has been for others, even though admirers of the KJV may be reluctant to admit it. In the genealogy of Christ given in the first chapter of Matthew's Gospel we are told (v. 6) that "David the king begat Solomon of her *that had been the wife* of Urias." One of the copies of the KJV in my possession uses italics in this verse; another does not. Inevitably, something had to be added, so the added words were supplied from the history recorded in 2 Samuel 11. The Greek original merely says that "David begat [that is, was the father of] Solomon out of her [clearly feminine] of Uriah." Much history is obviously condensed in these few words. But taken as they stand they do not read as English; nor would they mean anything to a person reading the Scriptures without any biblical background.

The point is simply that here—and in many other places —Bible translators have no choice but to add words or alter constructions in order to complete the ellipses, that is, to fill in the gaps. Translation without such elaboration would be meaningless; translation with it becomes—like it or not—paraphrase.

CHAPTER 4

TWO WAYS OF TRANSLATING

I F ALL TRANSLATIONS can be classified on a continuum ranging from various forms of "literal" at one extreme to various types of "idiomatic" at the other, one might easily assume that the difference between the two extremes is merely one of *degree*. One could also suppose that there is basically only one way of translating and that differences reflect not a different approach to the translation task but only a different degree of faithfulness.

Many authorities in Bible translation, however, see the difference as not one of degree but of kind. In other words, there are two different approaches to translating. One emphasizes *form* and the other stresses *content*. Newman calls them the "old way" and the "new way,"[1] but the adjectives *old* and *new* refer more to methodology than to chronology. One finds even new translations of the Scriptures that are largely based on the "old" (form-oriented) method of translating; conversely, some rather old translations actually embodied many of the "new" (content-oriented) ways of translating even before the two approaches were generally defined.

Form-Oriented Translation

The old way of translating is, basically, the traditional way, the primary system by which the Bible was translated into most languages until quite recent times. The method reached its peak in the nineteenth century.

Those who follow this method assume that languages are largely alike, at least enough so that a translator can move directly from one language to another. The approach is generally called *formal correspondence,* in which the word *formal* is used in the sense of being concerned with the outward *form* of something as distinguished from its content. In other words, the emphasis is on the form of the original or source language, with the assumption that the form can largely be carried across into the new or receptor language. The language one translates *from* is called the source language, the language one translates *into,* the receptor language.

There was a time when the receptor language was also known as the "target" language. In recent years that term has been avoided as misleading because it suggests shooting a communication at a target and treats communication as a one-way street instead of expecting a response in the receiver. The word *receptor,* on the other hand, stresses the fact that the message has to be "decoded" by those to whom it is directed. In other words, communication is inadequate and incomplete unless it is "received" (that is, understood).

According to the "old" method, a translator's chief attention is on the *source* language and everything is done to make the receptor language conform to *it.* That is why, incidentally, older generations of theological students learning Greek appreciated the ASV of 1901 so much. By memorizing it they could easily translate the Greek since the ASV represented so faithfully, in a literal, word-for-word fashion, what the Greek had said. For the most part, nouns were translated by nouns, verbs by verbs, and every *and* in Greek had to be accounted for in English. For example, count the *and*'s in the first chapter of Mark in the KJV (84), the English Revised Version (RV), the ASV, RSV, NASB and even NIV. In part this explains why the NASB, which follows the 1901 principles of the ASV, praises that older version as "the Rock of Biblical Honesty."

Another good example of formal correspondence may be seen in 2 Corinthians 10:14-16 in the ASV: "For we stretch not ourselves overmuch, as though we reached not unto you: for we came even as far as unto you in the gospel of Christ: not glorying beyond *our* measure, *that is,* in other men's labours: but having hope that, as your faith groweth, we shall be magnified in you according to our province unto *further* abundance, so as to preach the gospel even unto the parts beyond you, *and* not to glory in another's province in regard of things ready to our hand." No wonder Nida remarks about this passage: "The words may be English, but the grammar is not; and the sense is quite lacking."[2] Further, the KJV of nearly three centuries earlier and the RSV of a half century later make very little improvement over what we have here.

The words are indeed English—there is not a difficult word among them— but hand them to people on the street and ask them what they mean. Then you will understand what I meant by saying that communication is not a one-way street. If there is no response—and, remember, even rejection is a form of response—there has been no communication.

Much of the church's witness—evangelism, if you prefer—has been vitiated, not because it has been insincere or halfhearted, but because it has been couched in a language that common people no longer use (if, indeed, they ever did use it). Howard Hendricks labels this our "fog index" and says:

We evangelicals have a special talent for a high fog index in our speech. . . . We can partly blame King James' antiquated English for the high fog index, but much of the fault is twentieth-century Christian. We haven't made the effort to translate spiritual language into everyday situations, and our Sunday jargon is forced to take a rest the other six days of the week. We need a graphic, simple language that will get a hearing in the marketplace.

Some of our words are simply too big . . . people can understand us better if we use simple words. Certain words are vital, but they are clear only if they are explained. Such terms as *saved, redemption, propitiation, the deeper life, total depravity,* and many others belong to a specialized vocabulary which must be defined.[3]

Even the translators of the KJV in their "Preface on Translation" made it clear that one of their purposes was "the saving of soules. Now what [they ask] can be more available thereto, than to deliver God's booke unto God's people in a tongue which they can understand? . . . How shall men meditate in that which they cannot understand? How shall they understand that which is kept close in an unknown tongue?"[4]

It is because that very version which proclaimed so high a goal no longer speaks the language of ordinary people that we are constantly confronted with new versions that purport to do so. Kubo and Specht note that "to the average man of today the language of the KJV seems strange and foreign. There is therefore danger that the Bible may seem to modern man to be something out of date and irrelevant."[5]

In a similar vein the preface of *The Twentieth Century New Testament* declared that "The retention . . . of a form of English no longer in common use is liable to give the impression that the contents of the Bible have little to do with the life of to-day."[6] That is exactly the impression that many people now have.

Every example I could give of formal correspondence

translation would simply reinforce the point that, for the most part, it does not communicate to the ordinary person today, if indeed it ever did. Ronald Knox warns us: "Constantly, then, you have to be on the look-out for phrases which, because you have so often met them in the Bible, read like English, and yet are not English. Many of them, beginning life as Bible English, have even crept into the language: 'to give a person the right hand of fellowship' [Gal. 2:9], for example."[7]

Commenting on the "double heart" of Psalm 12:2 (ASV), he notes that it doesn't make sense except as "an abnormal anatomical condition, or an obscure kind of convention at bridge."[8] Moreover, "there are hundreds and hundreds of other Hebraisms which we do not notice, because we have allowed ourselves to grow accustomed to them. We should have thought it odd if we had read in *The Times* 'General Montgomery's right hand has smitten Rommel in the hinder parts' [compare Ps. 78:66]; but if we get that sort of thing in the Bible we take it, unlike Rommel, sitting down. 'Mr. Churchill then opened his mouth and spoke' [Mt. 5:2]—is that English? No, it is Hebrew idiom clothed in English words."[9]

Obviously, the person Knox had in mind when he said "we" and "you" is one interested enough to read the Bible. The people who do not read it care even less. If we hope to communicate with—note that I said *with*, not *to*–them, then we have to make the effort to put the Bible in a language they can understand.

To the Christian the Bible is the Word of God. But though the Word is *God's* the language in which it comes to us is *man's*. It is of utmost importance therefore that we express God's message in words to which men and women today can relate. For the most part, formal-correspondence translations fail to fulfil this objective. They perpetuate the impression that the Bible is irrelevant, written for "somebody else, somewhere else," but not for twentieth-century people. The question is not resolved by asserting

"But that's what the Hebrew (or Greek) says!" Maybe it does. But what we have to ask is, How would the author have said it if he had been speaking *our language?*

Content-Oriented Translation

Form-emphasizing translation—the "old way" of translating— sought to establish "techniques for moving from one set of surface structures to another, with the least possible interference or distortion"; in contrast, content-emphasizing translation—the "new way"—recognizes that

> instead of going directly from one set of surface structures to another, the competent translator actually goes through a seemingly roundabout process of analysis, transfer, and restructuring. That is to say, the translator first analyzes the message of the *source* language into its simplest and structurally clearest forms, transfers it at this level [here is where we said that paraphrase comes into the picture], and then restructures it to the level in the *receptor* language which is most appropriate for the audience which he intends to reach.[10]

The label given to this type of translation nowadays is "dynamic equivalence" (in contrast to "formal correspondence"). What it means is that one tries to produce in the reader or hearer in the receptor language the same reaction to the message that the original author sought to produce in the immediate readers or listeners. It assumes that the original message was natural and meaningful and that the grammatical structure and words used were not discouragingly difficult but that people used them in their everyday lives.

Koine Greek

Until Adolf Deissmann's remarkable discovery in 1895, the language of the New Testament appeared practically unparalleled in Greek literature. For example, there is a considerable contrast between New Testament Greek and the Atticism of the same period embodied in literary works that attempted to recapture or mimic classical Attic Greek. As a result the New Testament language came to be called by scholars "tired Greek," "bad Greek," "Jewish Greek," "biblical Greek" or just plain "New Testament Greek." Deissmann recalls hearing a famous Greek scholar, Dr. Friedrich Blass of the University of Halle, even as late as 1894 declare, "The New Testament Greek should be recognized as something distinct and subject to its own laws."[11]

Similarly, in 1889 Hatch had declared that "Biblical Greek is thus a language which stands by itself,"[12] and Cremer[13] agreed with Richard Rothe, who had written in 1863 that "we may appropriately speak of a language of the Holy Ghost. For in the Bible it is evident that the Holy Spirit has been at work, moulding for itself a distinctively religious mode of expression out of the language of the country which it has chosen as its sphere, and transforming even conceptions already existing, into a shape and form appropriate to itself and all its own." Cremer concluded, "We have a very clear and striking proof of this in New Testament Greek."[14] In his monumental lexicon (1897) Thayer followed suit, listing 767 words as belonging to "Biblical Greek"[15] and adding that such a large list was "a restricted rather than an inclusive one."[16]

There were occasional hints to the contrary, however. Moulton and Milligan cite at least four writers who took a different stand with regard to the language of the New Testament.[17] Perhaps the most interesting of them was Professor Lightfoot of Cambridge. In 1863, the year that Rothe wrote of "a language of the Holy Ghost," Lightfoot reportedly said to his class: "You are not to suppose that the word [some NT word which had its only classical authority in Herodotus] had fallen out of use in the interval, only that it had not been used in the books which remain to us: probably it had been part of the common speech all along. I will go further, and say that if we could only recover letters that ordinary people wrote to each other without any thought of being literary, we should have the greatest possible help for the understanding of the language of the NT generally."[18]

That was a truly remarkable "prophecy," if we may call it that. As Moulton pointed out, however, two or three volumes of such documents were in existence all the time: "If he had only read them, I believe he would have anticipated by fifty years the discovery made in our time."[19]

These hints were not followed up, however, and it remained for Deissmann—at the time (1895) neither a university professor, nor a clergyman, but only a candidate for the ministry—to make one of the most important biblical discoveries of all time. Deissmann, then a private instructor at Marburg and later professor of New Testament at Berlin, was one day looking at a volume in the Heidelberg University library which contained selections from the recently discovered papyrological collections then at Berlin. Suddenly he recognized a great similarity between what he read there and what he was accustomed to reading in the Greek New Testament.

His first impression, confirmed by further study, proved to be the key to open the door to the language of the New Testament. Deissmann concluded that that language was not a poor "literary" imitation of the classical authors of the past, *nor* an esoteric, sacred language (strongly Semitic indeed), specially invented by the Holy Spirit for the writing of the New Testament. It was the nonliterary language of everyday life in the Greco-Roman world rather than the language of books or of a privileged few.[20]

Of his discovery Deissmann wrote: "To many it appeared as something perfectly obvious that Holy Scripture must be clothed in language at least as classical as that of Demosthenes or Plato, and assertions to the contrary were felt to be an outrage upon the Holy Ghost. We for our part are on the side of those who see beauty in the wild rose bush as well as in a Gloire de Dijon. What is natural is also beautiful."[21]

To find out what the culture of a civilization is like, one does not ordinarily look in the garbage dumps of its cities. Yet from such rubbish heaps of ancient Egyptian towns we have learned the most about the "grass roots" of the centuries immediately before and after the coming of Christ. Curiously enough, the ancient Egyptians did not burn the contents of their wastepaper baskets but emptied them on the city rubbish heaps. And even though they tore their letters across before disposing of them, they were not so mutilated as to be illegible.

The bulk of the papyrus finds which Deissmann and others began to study were nonliterary in character, and almost infinite in variety and contents. Included were legal documents of all sorts, receipts and bills, leases, marriage contracts and bills of divorce, wills, tax papers, minutes of judicial proceedings, denunciations, pawnbrokers' lists, records of lawsuits and so on. There were also business letters, letters of complaint, love letters, notes and exercise books of schoolboys, diaries, horoscopes and magic formulas. Hardly any phase of life was left unrevealed by these papyrus discoveries.

In 1912 D. S. Margoliouth reflected a very pessimistic view of the value of the papyri when he wrote in *The Expositor* (January 1912, p. 73) that "not one percent of those which are deciphered and edited with so much care tell us anything worth knowing."[22] Today, however, no one could argue that the discoveries are irrelevant, because nearly all phases of New Testament study have been illuminated, if not revolutionized, by those finds from the Egyptian sands. Because of them we now know that the New Testament is not a supramundane book written for some kind of creatures other than ourselves in some language other than that of human beings.

As a result of his discoveries Deissmann was able to reduce Thayer's 767 words supposedly found nowhere else but in biblical Greek to about 50, which amounted to no more than one per cent of the total New Testament vocabulary of nearly 5,000 words.[23] From the papyri and other sources he illustrated many of the so-called biblical words, some of which seem so self-evident that one wonders why there was ever any doubt about them. For example, he wrote: "One can scarcely repress a smile on discovering in Thayer's 'Biblical' list the word [*onikos*], 'of or belonging to an ass,' which seems anything but 'Biblical' or 'Christian,' though it is true that oxen and asses are animals mentioned in the Bible."[24]

Other examples, noted at random in his works, include such words as *endiduskō*, "I put on" (Mk. 15:17; Lk. 16:19), which he calls "a perfectly colourless expression, in no way deserving this sacred isolation."[25] Another is *himatizō*, "I clothe" (Mk. 5:15; Lk. 8:35), which he labels as "no less worldly than the last word."[26]

In short, what this means is that "Wycliffe only did for England what Matthew and Mark did for the Roman world. Christianity from its beginning spoke the tongue of the peasant."[27] It is surprising that it took so long for biblical scholars to reach the conclusions that Deissmann through a stroke of genius came to almost overnight. What is even more surprising is that today, over three-quarters of a century later, many still argue that Bible language ought to be somewhat mysterious, so that to translate it in a way that makes sense to the common person is somehow an offense to God. To be sure, the jargon labeled by Hendricks as the church's "fog index" is quite acceptable to those who seem to revel in every new translation in the formal-correspondence style. Such translations tell them what they already know (or suppose they know). But these translations say almost nothing to people who have never heard the message before.

In contrast, those who seek dynamic equivalence in translation attempt to produce in the receptor language the closest natural equivalent to the message contained in the source language, keeping in mind both the meaning and the style. They recognize, of course, that no translation can succeed one hundred per cent; every translation suffers some loss of information, some addition of information and possibly also some distortion of information. For all that, however, one can try to find the closest equivalence possible. Nida clarifies this outlook:

> By "natural" we mean that the equivalent forms should not be "foreign" either in form (except of course for such inevitable matters as proper names) or meaning. That is to say, a good translation should not reveal its non-native source. . . .
>
> It is recognized that equivalence in both meaning and style cannot always be retained—in the acrostic poems of the Old Testament, to cite an extreme example [thus, Psalm 119]. When, therefore, one must be abandoned for the sake of the other, the *meaning must have priority* over the stylistic forms.[28]

To take a simple example from my own experience, suppose someone who speaks Urdu comes to talk with me, but I find it difficult to hear him. I ask him what's wrong, and he replies, "My throat has sat down." On the level of formal correspondence, if I were translating for you what he said I would have to state it that obtusely. I know, however, that what he *means* is that he has lost his voice, or is hoarse. Hence, if I give you the dynamic equivalent of his remark, I will tell you that he says he has lost his voice. The former was a literal translation with which no teacher of grammar could quarrel; what it lacked was a "dynamic" quality that came across to me (and to you) as it should have *in our language.* It emphasized form rather than content.

It is at this point that the validity of a translation, any translation—call it translation or call it paraphrase—must be tested. It is easy to regard the former ("my throat has sat down") as "faithful" translation and the latter ("I've lost my voice" or "I'm hoarse") as paraphrase (as if "never the twain shall meet"). But this is undoubtedly because most of us do not understand what fidelity in translation really is. Beekman and Callow define "faithful translation" like this:

A translation which transfers the meaning and the dynamics of the original text is to be regarded as a faithful translation. The expression, *transfers the meaning,* means that the translation conveys to the reader or hearer the information that the original conveyed to its readers or hearers. The message is not distorted or changed [though the *form* may be]; it has neither unnecessarily gained nor lost information. The expression, *the dynamics,* means that (1) the translation makes a natural use of the linguistic structures of the r[eceptor] l[anguage] and that (2) the recipients of the translation understand the message with ease. The naturalness of the translation and the ease with which it is understood should be comparable to the naturalness of the original and the ease with which the recipients of the original documents understood them. Such a comparison of the dynamics of the original with that of a translation must bear in mind that the message may have been easier for the original recipients to understand because Greek was the language of both writers and readers, and they shared the same or similar cultures. Also in some cases they had heard the writer speaking. On the other hand, the message was not dependent upon these local advantages since the writers were not penning abstract theses or obscure philosophies but had a very practical aim in view; they wrote to be understood.[29]

Analysis, Transfer and Restructuring

It has not been my aim in this book to produce a "How to" manual on translation, but merely to state in broad terms the two major approaches to the task. Those interested in the mechanics of translation can consult such books as Wonderly's *Bible Translations for Practical Use* (1968), Nida and Taber's *The Theory and Practice of Translation* (1969) and Beekman and Callow's *Translating the Word of God* (1974).

I have so far dealt at length with the major concepts of

formal correspondence and dynamic equivalence, but certain other terms merit at least some consideration.

Analysis The first of these, *analysis,* is concerned with what the message in the source language actually means; that is, what did it mean to those who first heard or read it? This meaning has to be discovered by looking at the relationships between words, phrases and clauses. Does the phrase "the love *of* Christ" (2 Cor. 5:14), for example, mean Christ's love for me or my love for Christ? The *of* in this phrase is ambiguous, but the issue must be decided before the words can be translated. A similar instance of ambiguity confronts us in Galatians 2:20, where we read about "the faith *of* the Son of God." Does that mean his faith or my faith in him? It is not possible to translate these simple words meaningfully until we know what they mean; that is where grammatical analysis comes in.

In addition to the grammar and syntax of the source language, we also need to understand the meanings of the words. Note that I have used the plural form *meanings,* since a word has both referential (dictionary) meaning (this equals [more or less] that) and also connotative meaning (conveying emotion or feeling, which the reader or hearer will react to, either positively or negatively).

As for referential meaning, let us take the example of the word *sarx* in Greek. Its basic dictionary meaning is "flesh" and sometimes it is used in this sense in the New Testament (for example, Lk. 24:39). But it also has many other meanings as well, such as (among others) "a human being" (Jn. 1:14), "people" (Acts 2:17), "human nature" (Rom. 8:3 TEV) or "sinful nature" (Rom. 8:3 NIV), "world" (2 Cor. 10:3) and even "human point of view" (1 Cor. 1:26 TEV) or "human standards" (1 Cor. 1:26 NIV). With the exception of the Acts 2:17 passage (where we find "mankind") the NASB retains "flesh" in all these examples. It is obvious that no matter how we decide to translate a word we must determine this by an analysis of the context in which that word is found.

As far as connotative meaning is concerned, we must ask about the emotional impact on a person of a particular word. The words *mother, woman, lady* and *madam* might all refer to the same person. But each connotes something different, so that the choice in translation must be carefully made. For example, what was the connotation (impression) conveyed by Jesus' words to Mary in John 2:4 and again in John 19:26? By using the word *gunai* in Greek, was he being disrespectful? In English it might sound that way, since few of us call our mother *Woman, Lady* or *Madam*. The connotation in Greek, however, is far more favorable than it is in English. Consequently, the NEB and JBP make a shift in the referential meaning in order to give us something connotatively closer to the original. They have Jesus call Mary, *Mother*.

The TEV, NIV (first edition) and LB, sensing the problem, simply leave the word out and have Jesus speak directly to Mary without calling her anything. In its first edition the NIV does give a footnote showing the literal form and adding that this is "a polite form of address"; later editions include the phrase "Dear woman." The JB (Catholic retains the traditional "Woman," perhaps as an allusion to Genesis 3:15, to contrast her with the first Eve, the "mother of the living." The NASB, not surprisingly, also keeps the traditional form of address, "Woman."

Analysis, then, is the starting point in good translation; otherwise, one gets literalisms which either do not convey anything or convey the wrong thing. This is not a light matter, as Mundhenk points out:

> A translator who gives the wrong meaning in this way has fallen into a very common trap: he thinks that as long as he keeps the "same" words he cannot be too far wrong with the meaning. Instead, what he has done is not translation at all—he has put a new, and therefore wrong, message into the Bible. Whenever this happens, the problem has become very serious indeed.

Now what makes a translator put something in such literal form? In most cases I think there is one simple reason: *the translator does not understand what the original means.* Sometimes the translator knows that he does not really understand it, but he hopes that it will be safe enough just to "say what it says." So he puts down a literal word-for-word "translation." At other times a translator does not really understand the original, but thinks that he does understand it. . . .

No one can translate a sentence if he does not know what it means.[30]

Mundhenk might have added still another reason, as Nida does, namely, linguistic bias or linguistic fervor. What Nida means by this is that translators may have such an exaggerated respect for the source language—depending on their own views of inspiration—that they lean over backward in favor of formal correspondence, forcing the receptor language to conform.[31] The result? "A kind of translationese" which only God can fully understand!

Transfer   Another important term used by Bible translators who aim for dynamic equivalence is *transfer*. Transfer is essentially a subjective process that goes on in the minds of translators as they struggle in their role as "bridge" between the meaning of the source language and the various options open to them in expressing that meaning in the receptor language. (Remember the examples with "John hit Bill on the nose"?) At this stage in the process translators have to keep in mind not just the word (as if *A* in the source language equals *B* in the receptor language), not even just the sentence, but the paragraph and, in fact, the entire discourse. What is the *total* message the author wishes to convey? Not merely, What does he mean by this prepositional phrase? Translators do not see "verses" in isolation, as they are printed in the KJV and the NASB. Considering the relatively late arrival of chapter and verse numbering, they look at the total discourse and do not arbitrarily break it at Mark 8:38 (for example) but carry it on to chapter 9, verse 1. Nor do they stop at 1 Corinthians 10:33 but carry on through 11:1 in order to complete the sense.

More than that, they consider the type of literature they are translating. Is it prose or poetry? Will the language they are translating into permit certain texts to be expressed poetically, or will this form have to be sacrificed for the sake of the meaning? If they are rendering a "story," is it really an incident that occurred or only an illustration? How does the receptor language deal with these? In English, for example, the phrase "Once upon a time" does not mean literally what is *says;* it is a formula to tell us that what follows is a fairy tale and, actually, never happened.

Along comes an idiom such as "gird up the loins of your mind" (1 Pet. 1:13) or "cast the same in his teeth" (Mt. 27:44). The latter, however, is an idiom not of the Greek, which simply says "to reproach, upbraid, censure, denounce or insult, " but of *English*, going back at least as far as Coverdale (1535) and found in Shakespeare (1596), who writes (in *Henry IV*, v.ii.42) of "defiance in King Henries teeth." Will translators give these phrases literally (and therefore meaninglessly) or will they in the receptor language shift them to nonidiomatic form, such as "prepare your minds for action" (NIV) or "insulted [TEV]/taunted [NEB] him in the same way"? Surprisingly, even the LB in the Matthew passage continues to say, "And the robbers also threw the same in his teeth."

Translators must also look to cultural matters. When they read in Matthew 27:39 that those who passed by Jesus as he hung on the cross "wagging their heads" (KJV, NASB), they must ask if that is what people in the receptor culture do to express disapproval. Or might that action show approval among the people who will read the translation? How do *they* show disfavor? Even in English it is difficult to understand people "wagging" their heads (tails, maybe, but not heads). Heads are shaken (as TEV), tails are wagged—at least in the latter part of the twentieth century.

Another cultural problem is the matter of honorifics. In English *you* can be either singular or plural and may be applied to a president or a tramp. In many languages, however, there are several ways of addressing someone—all to be translated "you"—depending on how (in social status) you rank that person.

Then there is the matter of quotations. What if there are quotations within quotations within more quotations? Can they be expressed, or will the individual speakers have to be identified in order to make the message clear? The same might be asked where there is a string of *he*'s and *him*'s (for example, Jn. 12:39-43 RSV, NASB) or of *they*'s and *their*'s (for example, Judg. 3:6 RSV, NASB) where it is very difficult to tell who is doing or saying what and to whom. The matter is made even more complicated in some languages where the same word is used for *he/she/it* and *him/her/it.*

There are many passive verbs in our Bible. The Gospel of Matthew is full of them (as in the Sermon on the Mount) with such statements as "they shall be comforted" (5:4 KJV, NASB), "they shall be filled" (5:6 KJV), "they shall be called the children of God" (5:9 KJV) and others. In some languages it is not natural to use the passive form of the verb. The active is preferable, but to use it the various participants in the event will have to be named. Shall we say, "God will comfort them!" "God will satisfy them fully!" and "God will call them his children!" as the TEV does?

These and many other problems have to be struggled with and for the most part the struggle takes place in the translator's mind. If in the process of making the transfer a translator is able to convey some of the form of the original as well as the content and connotation of the message, then that is all to the good. But if not, content must take priority over form. The work of translation is indeed a mind-boggling business, not to be engaged in lightly or treated casually.

Restructuring   The third step, after analysis and transfer,

is called *restructuring*. Newman summarizes what is meant:
      This aspect, of course, relates very much to style, and
   one must always keep in mind the *intended audience*, in
   cluding both their educational and cultural back-
   grounds. The structure of the whole piece of writing
   must be one, with the relation of each part to the whole
   made clear in the most natural and appealing way, and
   yet in such a fashion as not to alter the emotional impact
   of the original document. Level of vocabulary, sentence
   length, complexity of clause and phrase structure, con-
   nectives, constructions designed for effect—these and
   many other matters must be constantly weighed by the
   translator as he tries to restructure in a way that will most
   naturally transfer the whole content of the message to
   his readers.[32]

Common Language

One of the key phrases used by Newman above is "the
intended audience." It is this consideration as much as anything else that distinguishes a good translation. In fact,
there is no such thing as a "good translation." "Good for
whom?" is the question we need to ask. It is not enough to
translate for "somebody out there." We have to know who
that somebody is. Is he or she a traditional churchgoer who
is already familiar with much of the Bible? Is the intended
reader a young person or a child, or a better-educated person, but all with little background in scriptural knowledge?
Should the translation be a simple, straightforward one for
the masses, or a simplified one for those who are just learning to read? The message in every case will be the same, but
the form will depend on the intended audience.

   Largely with his in mind, recent years have seen an increase in what are known as "common language" versions.
But it is important to clarify what is meant by common language. Some people misunderstand it to mean slang or low-
class, vulgar (in the sense of substandard) language, when it
does not actually mean that all.

Every language has what may be called different *levels* of expression, and these differ between the spoken and joint written forms. All of us, for example, are able to read and understand many more words than we actually use in our speech. A number of levels can be identified, depending on the language. At least three seem always to be found: (1) the language of the technician, specialist or professional (imagine this at the top of the scale); (3) vulgar language which occurs in every society, but which is usually found on the tongues of the less educated or illiterate (such language can be pictured at the bottom of the scale, and need not be "indecent" but simply colloquial or even substandard —"I seen him do it" and "Me and John went," as well as slang, are examples); and (2) between these, a range of language the specialist will accept (and use) and the less educated will understand (and also use). This area of overlap is known as common language. It is that form of the language known and used by all levels of the society in question.

An interesting illustration comes from the U.S. Income Tax Form 1040 for 1977. Previously, the question on page 1 regarding the Presidential Election Campaign Fund read: "Do you *wish* to *designate* $1 of your taxes for this fund? If joint return, does your spouse *wish* to *designate* $1?" (italics mine). For the first time the 1977 form simplified this by asking, "Do you *want* $1 to *go* to this fund? If joint return, does your spouse *want* $1 to *go* to this fund?" (italics mine). The meaning has not changed, but the form certainly has. The words *want* and *go* fall within the middle range of language which we call common, and are thus accessible to (that is, understood by) the masses of whatever educational level. No taxpayers, not even those with Ph.D.'s, will feel that such words as *want* and *go* are beneath them.

It is in the area of common-language English that the TEV has made a great contribution. Commenting on that, Kubo and Specht note that

by this is meant that part of the English language understood by people from all walks of life and all levels of education who can read and write English. Although no arbitrary limit is set on the vocabulary [of the TEV], a studious effort is made to keep the language simple and direct. The Bible must be made understandable not only to Christians with little formal education, but also to non-Christians who are unfamiliar with technical religious vocabulary. Not only must the language of the elite be avoided, but also slang. Regional and provincial expressions, as well as idioms, are kept to a minimum.[33]

Considering the discovery that the New Testament was written in everyday language, and the newly recognized importance of the receptor in genuine communication, it is not surprising that many Bible translators today emphasize the new rather than the old way of translating, in other words, stress content rather than form. Nor is it surprising that this trend brings them into disagreement with those who regard anything but literal or formal translation to be paraphrase. It is, in fact, impossible to analyze, transfer and restructure without paraphrasing at the level of the underlying kernel structures; and that, in turn, shows up at the final level of the surface structure. When it does not, the result is not English (or whatever language we are translating into), but Hebrew and Greek in English disguise.

Further, those who favor the traditional approach would do well to consider Nida's warning regarding the results of the two methods.

In practice F[ormal]-E[quivalence] translations tend to distort the message more than D[ynamic]-E[quivalence] translations, since those persons who produce D-E translations are in general more adept in translating, and in order to produce D-E renderings they must perceive more fully and satisfactorily the meaning of the original text. For the most part a translator who produces D-E renderings is quite aware of the degree of distortion, and because of greater conscious control of his work is able to judge more satisfactorily whether or not the results seem to be legitimate. On the other hand, a translator who produces strictly F-E renderings is usually not conscious of the extent to which his seemingly "faithful" translations actually involve serious distortions. This lack of awareness in F-E translating as to what is happening results in far more serious skewing [damage to the message] than is generally the case with D-E translating.[34]

CHAPTER 5

HOW MISSIONARIES HAVE HELPED

IN THE FIRST CHAPTER I pointed out that during the first fifteen centuries of the Christian era the Bible or some portion of it had been translated into only about thirty-three languages, and that even after eighteen centuries scarcely seventy-one languages contained anything of the Holy Scriptures. The best known (such as Latin, English, German, Dutch, Italian, Spanish and Swedish, to name a few), belonged to the Indo-European family of languages. In spite of their variety there was a certain underlying similarity that made it comparatively easy to bridge the gap between the biblical languages and the languages being translated into. Allowing that the Old Testament Hebrew was Semitic rather than Indo-European, at least the thought patterns of most of the translators were used to the kinds of declensions and conjugations, genders and syntax that overlap in many of these languages. Give or take a little, grammatical structures were even regarded by some as well-nigh universal.

However, with the dawn of the nineteenth century—the so-called missionary century—and the publication of the Scriptures in many new languages, as far removed as Bengali and Cherokee, Korean and Swahili, Aztec and Malay, the picture became far more complex than anyone had ever imagined. As Bible translators moved into areas using languages belonging to other great families of languages besides Indo-European, it became obvious that not all languages could be traced back to Latin or even to Sanskrit (also Indo-European). Only slowly did scholars come to acknowledge the ego- and ethnocentrism which regarded the inflected languages of Europe as the highest form of speech.

Even today most people think of some languages (those most like their own) as "civilized" and others as "primitive," meaning that they have "no grammar" (which *they* can detect) and "little vocabulary" (which *they* can understand). It does not occur to them that such beliefs reflect only *their* prejudice and ignorance, and not the ignorance of those whose languages they so casually judge.

The dawn of the modern missionary movement in the nineteenth century, and with it the proliferation of Bible translations, is significant in another respect. To understand that, we must go further back in history. Despite the outstanding work of such translators as Wycliffe, Luther and Tyndale and the "principles of translation" laid down by Etienne Dolet, most early Bible translators seemed bound mainly by one guiding rule. That rule might be called the principle of "brevity," thinking that to add to the number of words of, say, the Greek was to be unfaithful to the original. For example, "the preface to the Rhemish Testament accuses the Protestant translators of having in one place put into the text 'three words more . . . than the Greek word doth signify.' "[1]

Partly in reaction to such attitudes, seventeenth- and

eighteenth-century secular writers began to urge an un-restrained freedom when it came to translation. For example, in 1656 the poet Abraham Cowley justified his radical rendering of Pindar's *Odes* by saying: "If a man should undertake to translate Pindar word for word, it would be thought *one Mad-man* had translated another.... I have ... taken, left out, and added what I please; nor made it so much my aim to let the reader know precisely what he spoke, as to what was his way and manner of speaking."[2] In 1680 John Dryden, English poet laureate, justly criticized Cowley's radical approach, labeling his translations "imitations."

Because of such extremism in the direction of paraphrase (in its worst sense), the pendulum began to swing the other way in the nineteenth century. It was a period of "supersophistication," summed up by Nida in these words: "The classical revival of the 19th century and the emphasis upon technical accuracy, combined with a spirit of exclusivism among the intelligentsia, conspired to make that century as pedantic in its attitudes toward translation as it was toward many other aspects of learning."[3]

It is important to remember that a great many of the major "missionary translations" of the Scriptures were made in that century, often following the literal English translations of the same period—for example, the RV of 1881 and 1885 and, in the earlier part of the twentieth century, the ASV of 1901. Such versions are, to borrow the words of Savory about another work, a classic example of "primitive translation, verbally accurate, yet lacking in any other quality for which [they] may be commended."[4] They simply failed to communicate effectively.

With the twentieth century has come a tremendous change in the principles of translation which had remained more or less static for centuries. Thus Nida observes, "In the first place, new concepts of communication have developed in our shrinking world. Not only have semanticists and psychologists insisted that a message which does not communicate is useless, but advertisers and politicians, among others, have set a high premium upon *intelligibility*."[5]

In addition to the new concepts of what constitutes effective communication and a new appreciation of culture, the science of linguistics has also come into its own in our century. This vast field—including structural, socio- and psycholinguistics—may well replace many of the presuppositions of nineteenth-century classical philology.

Two movements that have applied the latest methods of structural linguistics to the special problems of Bible translation in our century are the Wycliffe Bible Translators (WBT), specializing particularly in minority languages and literacy around the world, and the United Bible Societies (UBS), dealing with both minority and major languages world wide. The latter is a conglomerate (in the nontechnical sense) made up of the Bible Societies of many countries: for example, the American Bible Society (ABS), the British and Foreign Bible Society (BFBS), and so on. Most of them have been in existence for many generations, The BFBS, for example, since 1804.

The WBT was founded by William Cameron Townsend, who had gone to the Indians of Guatemala at the age of twenty-one with a trunk full of Spanish-language Bibles. He soon learned not only that few of the Indian population knew Spanish, but that few even cared to learn it.

One day, after Townsend had offered a copy of the Bible to an Indian, he was rebuked with the words, "Why, if your God is so smart, hasn't he learned our language?" Clarence Hall, describing the incident, says, "Then and there, Townsend quit Bible distribution in favor of giving God another tongue."[6] For fifteen years Townsend literally "lived" with the Cakchiquel tribe, mastered their difficult language, reduced it to writing and slowly developed a simplified method for teaching *any* phonetically written language. He left Guatemala in 1932, racked with tuberculosis; but in the summer of 1934 along with an old missionary friend, Leonard L. Legters, he turned an abandoned farmhouse in the Arkansas Ozarks into a pioneer training camp "to train mission candidates in primitive-language reduction and Bible translating."[7] That program continues today, with several branches worldwide, as the Summer Institute of Linguistics (SIL).

The WBT and the UBS have each published an impressive number of technical works on linguistic subjects and Bible translation, including (by UBS) a quarterly journal called *The Bible Translator* (TBT) begun in 1950.

Without doubt, no other piece of literature has been translated into so many languages and in such varied cultures as has the Bible. Therefore, Bible translators—in former times, mostly missionaries; nowadays, often nationals—possess a wealth of linguistic information found nowhere else. One of the most prolific compilers of such linguistic and anthropological data relevant to the translation of the Bible is Eugene A. Nida, whose works I have frequently quoted. Nida's *God's Word in Man's Language* (1952), *Customs and Cultures* (1954) and other writings are replete with illustrations of the challenge and reward of taking the good news of Christ to (quite literally) "earth's remotest regions."

With the pace of Bible translating stepped up as never before, biblical linguists are anxious to assure that the *meaning* of the Bible gets across and thus seek to establish for their translators rules to guarantee this. They are anxious to move away from "literal translation," which, beginning with the Septuagint (a stiff, formal translation) has largely dominated Bible translation through the centuries. The demand for literalness most often comes from people not linguistically trained. The Bible *in translation* is treated like a "sacred cow" by many who "forget that the assignment of meaning to any term is done *by the receiving culture,* not by the culture of the language that is being translated."[8]

According to Nida, literalness in biblical translation— and the principle holds good for other types of translation as well—should give way to *flexibility.* Parker says that a translation should be "judged to be good or bad not in isolation but in relation to its effect on the audience. The purpose of the translator is to remain faithful to the source language, but so to shape it that the receptor will respond to the message within his culture in the same way that a person who speaks the original language responds within his."[9]

As translations secretary of the American Bible Society and translations research coordinator for the United Bible Societies, Dr. Nida, along with workers under the Wycliffe Bible Translators, shares a large responsibility for the new insistence that translation be carried out in *cultural context.*

The jacket of *God's Word in Man's Language* quotes a letter received at the American Bible Society's Bible House: "I would be so glad to help in the translating of the Bible, and so if you would send me a dictionary and a grammar of some of these primitive languages, I would be happy to dedicate my spare time to the translation of the New Testament."[10] Notwithstanding the sincerity and good intentions of the writer, the request could not be honored! Even if there were a dictionary and grammar—in many cases there is neither—Bible translation cannot be done in a cultural vacuum and in one's spare time.

When we look at the translation of any piece of literature, we can try to cross the barriers of time and culture in two opposite ways: either (1) we can carry today's reader back (or over) to the original, or (2) we can bring the original up (or over) to today's reader. The former is what is usually attempted in Bible translation; the latter is exemplified in Clarence Jordan's local-dialect version of the Scriptures called *The Cotton Patch Version,* which substitutes place names in the state of Georgia for biblical ones. Commenting on these two approaches, Nida points out that "by close attention to literal wording and formal correspondence one can be transported back to an earlier culture or off to some contemporary, but foreign, one. However, literalness and formal agreement do not let us feel really at home in such a strange literary land, nor do they actually help us to appreciate as we should how this same message must have impressed those who first heard it. Without some adjustments in form and content, at times even rather radical, no literary translation can fully accomplish its real purpose."[11]

After giving various definitions of "translation" in chapter two, I might have summarized by saying that translation is an equivalence of thought which happens to be expressed verbally in a variety of ways. The fact that identical equivalents generally do not exist emboldened Robert Graves to go so far as to say that "translation is a polite lie, but nevertheless a lie."[12] Why? Because even a simple word like *bread* will convey to different people different ideas of shape, color, size, weight, taste and so on. In other words, a people's culture and world view have as much to do with meaning as the bare words themselves have.

Mundhenk points out that "the very fact that we have a word in our own language usually means that it refers primarily to some modern thing. Even with words like *table, bread, bed, basket, well,* or *sandal,* all unquestionably correct words to use in a translation, the reader will often be picturing to himself item after item which would have looked decidedly queer to the Biblical characters."[13]

Granting that identical equivalents may be difficult to come by, we need not be so pessimistic in our view of translation as to call it a "lie." We can look for *near equivalents.* In that search we have essentially two choices, "formal equivalence" (or correspondence) and "dynamic equivalence," as explained in chapter four. The dynamic approach stresses the effect of the message on its hearers. In that way it "aims at complete naturalness of expression, and tries to relate the receptor to modes of behavior relevant within the context of his own culture; it does not insist that he understand the cultural patterns of the source-language context in order to comprehend the message,[14] though these may be helpful as follow-up or teaching material."

One of the chief sources of the trend toward the dynamic dimension has been the large number of crosscultural ("missionary") translations produced in recent decades.

To make a translation communicate effectively attention must be given, among other things to the following four considerations.

Functional Equivalents

One area of misunderstanding regarding translation relates to biblical terms for which a receptor language has no equivalent term. For example, consider the word *snow*. If the language being translated into belongs to a people in a hot, tropical climate who have never seen or heard of snow, how can one translate a verse such as Isaiah 1:18, "The LORD says, 'Now, let's settle the matter. You are stained red with sin, but I will wash you as clean as snow" (TEV)?

For one thing, such people may have heard of snow even though they may not have it in their own environment. Or they may have an equivalent idiom, "white as . . . ," enabling us to substitute something else that conveys whiteness (cleanness, purity) to them. Nida and Taber suggest "white as egret feathers" or "white as fungus" (if they have an especially white fungus)—provided these expressions are already idioms within the language.[15] When such idioms do not exist, they recommend a nonmetaphor such as "very, very white" (or pure). In no case where an idiom does not already exist, would they recommend that translators make up their own! Their job is to translate—to communicate, not to invent. The point is that snow as an object is not a crucial element here; it is the concept of cleanness or purity that is in focus, for which one can usually find an acceptable equivalent.

Consider an example from Matthew 20:3, where the KJV, ASV, JB, RSV, NASB and NIV all say that a landowner went out "about the third hour." Even in English the expression is meaningless unless translated as "about/at nine o'clock [in the morning]" (as in TEV, JBP and WB). In societies not bound by the clock one might have to make even a further adjustment, such as starting out with "early one morning" and then mentioning "three hours later" (NEB), "a couple of hours later" (LB) or some other time word which *is* used in that language. It makes no sense to talk about "the third hour" unless one explains "in relationship to what." If a version has provision for footnotes, such information can be given there; the translation of the text itself ought to be smooth and readable and in the most natural equivalent available.

In Matthew 8:8 a centurion tells Jesus that he is not worthy to have him come *under* his *roof,* an expression that makes sense—even if archaic sense—in English, as rendered in the KJV, ASV, JB, RSV, NASB, JBP and NEB. In the LB, TEV and WB, however, the phrase is rendered "into my house [or home]." The point is that it means "the place where I live"—which may be a tent, courtyard, jungle clearing, or some other abode not properly associated with a "roof." For such people it would be better to shift to a cultural equivalent that suggests the place where they live. A good question to ask in such cases is, If the centurion happened to live in their village or camp or jungle or desert, what would he have said to Jesus *there?* In fact, *centurion* might better be rendered "army officer" or "military officer," since the word as it stands is not clear to most people.

Translators do not have carte blanche to change or adapt anything that suits their fancy. Such free-for-all paraphrase is rightly objected to. Any proposed change or cultural adaptation that does violence to the original is not justified. Translators must not misinterpret the point of the original message, nor add information from any source other than the text, especially from some other foreign cultural environment.

Consider Luke 13:11 in JBP, for example, where Phillips says, "In the congregation was a woman who for eighteen years had been *ill from some psychological cause;* she was bent double and was quite unable to straighten herself up" (italics mine). The text says that the woman's condition was the result of the effects of a "spirit." TEV and WB both give the translation "evil spirit" but most other translations simply reproduce the word *spirit*. Arndt and Gingrich's *Lexicon*, which gives twenty-nine subdivisions of various usages of the word *spirit*, classifies the Luke 13:11 example under the heading "evil spirits."[16] It is true that use of the simple word *spirit* in today's English is too ambiguous to communicate much. We may argue that twentieth-century people do not speak of evil spirits, yet we must admit that first-century people *did*. Moreover, not all twentieth-century people reject the notion of Satan and evil spirits. The context says the woman's condition was due to effects of an indwelling evil spirit. Thus Phillips by his translation ("some psychological cause") brings in a cultural interpretation that is absent from, if not downright foreign to, the intent of the text.

In similar fashion the LB's reference in Matthew 20:3 to a "hiring hall" sounds too reminiscent of a local union in the United States, something quite foreign in the original culture and to many of the cultures into which the message will be translated. As another example, for the great wedding dinner described in Matthew 22, the king is said (in the LB) to have sent servants to tell the invited guests, "Everything is ready and the roast is in the oven. Hurry!" (v. 4). This may suggest to an American audience a homey Sunday afternoon dinner, but anyone who has attended a wedding feast in the Middle East (and many other parts of the world) will recognize that a "roast in the oven" would not be enough to provide even hors d'oeuvres for the crowd likely to be there.

Building Redundancy

Beside looking for functional equivalents to communicate effectively, a crosscultural translator will inevitably have to "build in redundancy," that is, to "draw out" the message of the original, giving additional information that the original readers had but today's readers do not have. He or she does this, *not* by introducing *new* information foreign to the context but rather by stating *explicitly* for today's readers what was given only *implicitly* in the text. A few examples will demonstrate this important principle.

Matthew 2:1 mentions that Jesus was born "in Bethlehem of Judea." Perhaps the English-speaking world by long association has the knowledge that Bethlehem is a town and that Judea is a province or region; the TEV, however, builds in redundancy by saying, "Jesus was born in *the town of* Bethlehem of Judea" (the words in italics not being in the Greek). That interpolation is not a case of eisegesis—putting into the text a meaning that is not already there—because no one reading the message for the first time would have had the slightest doubt that *that* is what was meant. Many civilizations today do not have the historical or geographical background to understand a word like Bethlehem. Such a "foreign" word does not by itself reveal whether it refers to a person, place or thing.

Mark 1:12 gives us another instance of implied information that needs to be made explicit. The KJV says, "And immediately the spirit driveth him into the wilderness." In many societies a similar reference to a "spirit" would suggest only a demon or evil spirit, but it is reasonably certain that what is meant here is the Holy Spirit. This is clarified in English by the convenience of capitalization—so, "Spirit" in many modern versions (as the TEV, NEB, NIV and even NASB, as well as ASV and RSV). But what about languages that have no system of lower- and upper-case letters? And even if they do, what about the many, perhaps the majority, around the world who do not themselves read but merely *hear* the Word read to them? It would not be out of place here to "build redundancy" into the text by adding the word *Holy*. The verse would then refer clearly to the Holy Spirit since he is the one who is meant. Strangely enough—was it an oversight?—even the KJV here does not capitalize the word *spirit*.

On the same occasion, we read (in Mt. 4:5) that the devil

took Jesus up into "the holy city." To many people that phrase would not mean anything. To some it might mean a city or place sacred to *them*. The TEV says plainly, "to Jerusalem, the Holy City," the word *Jerusalem* being added to make explicit to today's reader what was implicit to the original reader.

Many other examples of legitimate expansion could be presented. "Jordan" is often mentioned in the Gospels, once (Mk. 1:5) specifically referred to as "the River Jordan" but generally (as Jn. 1:28) with the word *river* omitted. For today's readers, who could conceivably associate the word with the nation Jordan, it is appropriate to include the word *river* along with the name, as the TEV does. Many societies in the world for whom the Scriptures are being translated would not understand *Jordan* standing by itself without further definition.

Pronouns must often be changed to nouns or sentences restructured to avoid ambiguity by making explicit what was implicit in the original. Thus Mark 1:19 in the KJV says, "He saw James the son of Zebedee, and John his brother." Does the *his* refer to James or to Zebedee? Was John the brother of James or the brother of Zebedee? Those with biblical knowledge know the answer. But a translator cannot always (in fact, can seldom) assume such familiarity on the part of readers. Although many, even modern, versions leave the verse ambiguous, the TEV and LB both clear it up but in different ways. The LB omits the fact that they were brothers, since (as worded) this would be obvious anyhow: "He saw Zebedee's sons, James and John." The TEV retains the fraternal relationship explicitly and renders the verse: "and saw two other brothers [besides Simon and Andrew, v. 16], James and John, the sons of Zebedee."

Although the principle was not specifically stated in their day, the translators of the KJV of 1611 obviously, even if sparingly, believed in building redundancy into their text. This is shown, as I mentioned earlier, by the words they italicized. Such words, though not found in the original Hebrew and Greek but clearly implied, were actually required in order to make "good English."

In all of these instances building redundancy results in a translation that is longer than the original. That is characteristic of paraphrase in its acceptable sense of saying the same thing in other words. In fact, as Nida and Taber state:

> There is a tendency for all good translations to be somewhat longer than the originals. This does not mean, of course, that all long translations are necessarily good. It only means that in the process of transfer from one linguistic and cultural structure to another, it is almost inevitable that the resulting translation will turn out to be longer.
>
> This tendency to greater length is due essentially to the fact that one wishes to state everything that is in the original communication but is also obliged to make explicit in the receptor language what could very well remain implicit in the source-language text, since the original receivers of this communication presumably had all the necessary background to understand the contents of the message. Moreover, there seems to be a relatively fixed tendency for languages to be approximately 50 percent redundant.[17]

Just how much redundancy a translator will add in a given instance depends on the nature of the audience he or she is translating for. As I have already pointed out, different audiences have different needs and different capacities to receive, understand and interpret the message. Some bitter critics of the *Good News Bible* (TEV), for instance, might temper their objections if they realized that the translation was actually produced for those who speak English as a second language—in other words, for those who are not that much at home in English because it is not their mother tongue. Further, the remarkable reception of this translation among the public at large (whose mother tongue *is* English) should say a lot to those who feel that only the King James Version, or something very close to it is worthy of the name *translation*. God's Word was given to be read, understood and acted on, not just to be revered and dusted off!

Communication Load

A third area of importance to which crosscultural translations have called attention is known as communication load. It is possible to have a lexically intelligible and grammatically correct translation that is still so "beyond" the reader or hearer that he or she cannot follow it. Conversely, it is possible to have one so simple or uninteresting that a reader or hearer will not bother with it at all. How can we account for this?

According to communication theory (specifically, information theory), any discourse has two important measurements, its length and its difficulty. A discourse that is prepared properly, that is, "encoded" to meet the needs of a specific group of receptors (whether children, young people, uneducated adults or educated adults), will have a component of difficulty approximately equal to the capacity of the receptors to take it in, that is, to "decode" it. In messages translated (or encoded) literally, word for word (as in formal-correspondence translations), the difficulty of comprehension is increased. Why? Because the receptors do not have the capacity to take in (or decode) such a message, since they do not have the same common information the original receptors had. Both their language and culture are different.

The problem, then, is to make some change so that the message we translate is approximately equal to the capacity of the receptors. How can we do it? One way is to increase the capacity of the receptor. Missions and churches in the past have largely worked along this line: they have tried to *teach* people so that the people would be used to such traditional biblical terminology as, for example, *sanctification, saved, flesh, repent, blood,* and *forgiveness*. The difficulty is that too many are outside the pale of our teaching and there is too much to teach. It is not practical to assume that all the people who buy a Bible will also get themselves a dictionary or a commentary to explain it. Besides, how can we *teach* people unless we first *reach* them?

A second way to match the message with the capacity of the receptors is to adjust the shape of the message. It is as if we had a certain number of items to pack into a suitcase for a trip. We have two suitcases of identical capacity, one is short and fat, the other longer but not as deep. Although the volume of the two bags is the same, some items may not fit into the short, stubby one. If we rearrange them all in the longer, shallower one, nothing is lost or left out. We still take on our trip all we had intended to—we just pack it into a case with a different shape.

I am not implying that some people have smaller capacities—in one African language (Zulu) there are 120 ways of describing how to walk. (How many can you think of in English?) Nor am I implying that Europeans or Americans have larger capacities. All of us have a large capacity for certain things in our own experience but much smaller capacity for other things. A medical doctor, for instance, may need a lot of simple explanations when a mechanic is telling him why his car motor doesn't work; the mechanic may need the same when the doctor tries to explain to him why he has high blood pressure. Both are "smart" in some things and "not so smart" in others, depending on their experience and background.

So, since it is not possible for translators to train or teach all of the people who are going to read their translation, they have little choice. If they want to communicate, they must adjust the shape of the message (or rearrange the baggage) so that it all comes across in the most natural way.

I have already described some of the ways translators can do that. They can give cultural or functional equivalents: thus *temple* can become "house of God" or "place of worship," *the third hour* can become "nine o'clock [in the morning]," *sabbath* can become "the [Jews'] day of rest and worship." Instead of trying to give a currency exchange rate for a *denarius* (which is bound to fluctuate with inflation) the translator can simply relate it to "the amount of money a common laborer earns in one day." The translation should not imply any fixed amount since that will vary from time to time and from place to place. Someone has pointed out that ordinary laborers in the U.S. earn far more (in functionally equivalent terms) than either first-century Jewish or twentieth-century Third World laborers. For that matter, they earn more than their fathers or mothers did in the U.S. a generation before.

A translator can also use simple words (*buy* instead of *purchase, teach* instead of *educate, try* instead of *endeavor, get* instead of *acquire,* and so on). It is worth noting that although the easier word is often shorter it is not always so. Compare the two words *sick* and *ill* (at least in American usage) or *animal* and *beast.* The longer ones are definitely more common.

The connotative meaning of a word plays an important part in its choice or rejection. So *belly* (as in 1 Cor. 6:13) is generally avoided nowadays in favor of something like *appetite* (as in LB) or *stomach* (as in JBP, TEV, WB). The word *belly,* though understood, seems to be *below* the level of acceptability by all classes and can therefore not be included in "common language." For similar reasons, the word *ass* (as in Mt. 21:2, 7), though only three letters long and given in the KJV and even the RSV, is replaced nowadays by the six-letter word *donkey* (NEB, NIV, NASB, JBP, JB, LB, WB, CBW and TEV)—twice the length but much more acceptable.

One also needs to beware of too much dependence on word counts or frequency lists prepared to show the "basic" vocabulary of a language. A 1,000-word list for English, for example, does not give the words *onion, tooth, stomach* or *elbow,* to name just a few. Yet these are common words for which it would be difficult to find suitable substitutes.

We have already observed how important it is for the context to determine the meaning assigned to a word. Hence a term like *sarx* in Greek is not invariably translated "flesh," which, as a matter of fact, it usually does not mean.

Translations generally end up being longer than the original because of built-in redundancy. But careful translations break up long sentences into shorter ones to fit the capacity of the intended readers or hearers. Ephesians 1:3-14, for example, in the original Greek is all one sentence; translators need not feel bound to render it as one in a receptor language. They should ordinarily break it up into several sentences, making it longer but adding to its ease of comprehension. Hebrews 10:19-22 is another long sentence in the KJV which the TEV breaks into four sentences and the LB into three. In the Urdu language the words in the passage total eighty-seven. And because the structure of Urdu requires the principal verb to come at the end of a sentence, the key word is reserved for position number eighty-seven. Imagine keeping eighty-six words full of information in limbo, as it were, until the readers get all the way to the end of a sentence to find out what is expected of them.

I sometimes illustrate this problem by playing a mathematical trick on people. I tell them, rather quickly and with no pauses for them to catch their breath, that I want them to "square 15, multiply by 4, divide by 10, subtract 89, and tell me the answer." Usually by the time I am halfway through they are either saying "Hold on!" or are searching in their pocket or purse for a pencil and paper in order to decode it. The answer is "1"; but the point is that the average person cannot keep so much information in mind before decoding what it means. This is the predicament of unfamiliar readers of the Bible. To communicate, translators must adjust the form or shape of the message to the capacity of their intended audience.

Attention must be paid to the complexity of single utterances as well as to their length. Recall that "kernels" are the main ideas underlying the "surface structure" of a message. Quite apart from the choice of words, a sentence is difficult or not, depending on whether the kernels are visible or hidden (embedded). Jacob Loewen of the United Bible Societies has a helpful way of illustrating this point. I will adapt his suggestion to a sentence of my own making: "The man who fixed our car which after several years of good service broke down only a month ago on the very day that my sister who lives in Oregon arrived in order to visit us came for his money." It is not the *words* that are difficult or the fact that there are forty of them—they are all "common [enough] language"—it's the way they are put together, with the kernels (main ideas) hidden in a structure requiring a reader or listener to keep too much information in mind before getting to the point.

How can we simplify such a sentence? One way, of course, is to break it up into several sentences. Another way is to keep it as one sentence but bring the kernels out into the open where they are visible rather than hidden. For example: "We paid the man / who fixed our dependable car / which broke down a month ago / when my sister from Oregon arrived/to visit us." The sentence now consists of twenty-four words and each unit (marked off by a /) is complete up to that point so there is no overload on memory or comprehension. Even someone who can't read would be able to understand a sentence like that.

To get at the underlying kernels that make up a sentence, Bible translators learn to recast expressions so as to bring out the actual (not surface or superficial) relationships between words. In the process their entire "universe" of experience is divided up into four categories and everything fits into one or another of these. There are *objects* (things or entities), *events* (actions, happenings or processes), *abstracts* (qualities, quantities and degrees of the first two classes) and *relationals* (words showing the meaningful connections between the other three groups).

Psychologists and linguists have found that the more highly educated a person is the more he or she is likely to use sophisticated, higher-level transformations which in many instances end up as nouns (what I have here called objects—although they may actually be events expressed in abstract form).[18] Similarly, the less educated a person is the more his or her speech will be made up of verbs (here called events). Moreover, it has been observed that restructuring sentences to the level of the kernels often brings out a verbal idea which on the surface-structure level appeared as a noun. The surface structure is more difficult to comprehend than the kernel structure and "the fact that languages agree far more on the level of the kernels than on the level of the more elaborate structures . . . means that if one can reduce grammatical structures to the kernel level, they can be transferred more readily with a minimum of distortion."[19]

Consider the example of Mark 1:4 from the RSV: "John . . . [preached] a baptism of repentance for the forgiveness of sins." Looking at this sentence from the viewpoint of English there is only one verb, "preached." *John, baptism, repentance, forgiveness* and *sins* are all nouns. But the only real object (that is, tangible thing) in the sentence is *John.* The rest of the words refer to "events"; thus, John *preaches,* John *baptizes,* people *repent,* God *forgives,* people *sin.* Such analysis (here oversimplified but explored in detail in Nida and Taber[20]) provides the framework and justification for the TEV's rendering of the passage: "So John appeared in the desert, baptizing and preaching. 'Turn away from your sins and be baptized,' he told the people, 'and God will forgive your sins.' " Retaining the essential message of the original, the form has been simplified (paraphrased) to make it fit the demands of communication load and the capacity of the receptors.

Obligatory Features
This century's crosscultural translations have also brought

to light what are known as "obligatory features." Such features are in contrast to "optional" ones which depend on the will (or style) of the translator. Thus one may begin Matthew 2:1 with "When Jesus was born in Bethlehem..." (as most translations) or "After the birth of Jesus in Bethlehem..."; the form chosen in English is optional. Either makes good sense, though the verbal rendering is easier and more "common" because the word *birth,* on the surface a noun (hence, an object) is really an event. The difference is basically one of style.

But there are many situations in Bible translation where one does not have a choice; the receptor language *requires* a certain form, making it obligatory for the translator.

Many languages require verbs to come at the *end* of clauses and sentences, whereas in the biblical languages they need not. In English we normally put qualifying words *before* those they modify, as "a beautiful house," "an angry man" or "a difficult lesson." But in many languages such words have to *follow* the word they modify: "a house beautiful" (which in English has almost become acceptable because of the magazine by that name), "a man angry" and "a lesson difficult." The word order of the receptor language is the determining factor.

As for gender and number, many languages follow grammatical rather than the natural gender to which we are accustomed in English. Others indicate gender only by context, if at all. There is no reason, at least to a layperson, why the word for gardener in Urdu looks like a feminine word but actually (and naturally) is masculine, or why the word for a necklace sounds like a masculine noun but is actually feminine. Nor is there any apparent reason why *car* in that language is treated as feminine but *motor* is masculine, especially since both words (borrowed from English) are used for the same object, the automobile. In one language with which I am familiar, nouns are pluralized unless they already have a modifier such as a number which already shows plurality (thus, "four chair," since the *four* tells us that the word is plural without our having to pluralize it). Yet for nonhuman objects (for example, flowers) even if the word is pluralized the verb remains singular. Those who translate the Scriptures must therefore be prepared to bend the restructured message into the grammatical and syntactical patterns of the receptor language, not insist on making it conform to the Hebrew or Greek forms.

Some languages have no passive voice at all for verbs; hence passive constructions in the original must be changed to actives in the receptor language. This is no great problem where, for example, we read that "Jesus . . . was baptized by John" (Mk. 1:9), since it is easy to say that "John baptized Jesus." Where the agent is not mentioned, however, (as in many of the beatitudes and other passages in Matthew), the implied agent(s) must be supplied.

In some languages it is not possible to speak of *father* and *son* without some form of possessing or identifying word, such as "my father" or "his son." What does one do with the many instances, particularly in the Gospel of John, where Jesus refers to "the father" and "the son"? In one language I have worked in, it is necessary to clarify by saying "the heavenly father," "my father" or "God the Father"; not to do this would violate the limitations set by the receptor language.

In English if we use two negatives together the result is a positive. But in many languages a double negative only adds emphasis but does not remove the negative idea.

In our language we love with the *heart*. In some languages, however, that would make no sense since they love with the *liver*, the *abdomen* or even the *throat*.[21] To us, the hole through which we put the thread of a needle is the *eye;* other peoples around the world refer to it as the *ear*, the *face*, the *nostril*, the *hole* or even the *foot*.[22]

Every language has ways of indicating connections and transitions. I have already noted that the Semitically influenced Greek writers of the New Testament had a tendency to use the connective *and* far more often than we need to (as in Mk. 1). We need not sit in judgment on them, however; our job is to employ in the receptor language only those forms of connection and transition appropriate for the style of literature we are translating (narrative, illustrative, doctrinal, poetic and so on). In other words, although it is possible to translate every *and* in Mark 1 by an *and* in some other language, the result is often ludicrous. It is amusing even in English. Again, we have to restructure the final text according to what is permissible in the *receptor* language, seeking an equivalence of meaning regardless of the final form it has to take.

The writings of Bible translators in recent years have alerted Christians in Western countries to some rather novel renderings of Scripture in languages far removed from their own. Some seem to regard that as what one must expect when translating the Word of God for "primitive" peoples. For themselves they will have none of it, however. In a far-off jungle or desert enclave people may need to have the Word paraphrased—but not Westerners steeped for centuries in Indo-European classics! Thus the tolerance—even enthusiasm—shown in conservative circles for crosscultural translations is not always extended to excellent Bible translations much closer to home. The best some Christians can say of translations in English or other Western languages that communicate admirably to modern men and women, is that they are "paraphrases," a pejorative word in their vocabulary.

Some of the finest examples of translation today, revealing a thorough understanding of what translation is all about, are found in the Third World, or at least outside the Anglo-American sphere. Those translators, seldom bound by a tradition of either indifference or resistance to change, were free to follow their consciences and proven translation principles.

J. B. Phillips, in the introduction to his new revised edition of *The New Testament in Modern English,* sums up those principles in the following way:

There seem to be three necessary tests which any work of transference from one language to another must pass before it can be classed as good translation. The first is simply that it must not sound like a translation at all. If it is skilfully done, and we are not previously informed, we should be quite unaware that it *is* a translation, even though the work we are reading is far distant from us in both time and place. That is a first, and indeed fundamental test, but it is not by itself sufficient. For the translator himself may be a skilful writer, and although he may have conveyed the essential meaning, characterisation and plot of the original author, he may have so strong a style of his own that he completely changes that of the original author. . . . I would therefore make this the second test: that a translator does his work with the least possible obtrusion of his own personality. The third and final test which a good translator should be able to pass is that of being able to produce in the hearts and minds of his readers an effect equivalent to that produced by the author upon his original readers. Of course no translator living would claim that his work successfully achieved these three ideals. But he must bear them in mind constantly as principles for his guidance.[23]

Some relatively modern translations of the Scriptures show little evidence of regard for the high ideals Phillips has laid down. They reflect concern more for source languages than for receptor languages and more for tradition than for communication.

CHAPTER 6

RESOLVING THE DEBATE

F ROM WHAT I HAVE SAID so far, two points should be obvious: (1) it is seldom possible to translate literally, word for word, without making adjustments in the receptor language which inevitably constitute some degree of paraphrase; and (2) translators are not at liberty to make just any changes that suit their fancy, but must make adjustments according to the demands of the receptor language and in faithfulness to the intent of the original author.

Paraphrase Inevitable
Let us look at a well-known, straightforward verse in the Bible which seems so simple that there could be no doubt about how it should be translated, the first verse of John's Gospel. The traditional rendering is, "In the beginning was the Word, and the Word was with God, and the Word was God" (KJV, ASV, RSV, JB, NASB, NIV). A literal, word-

for-word rendering of the Greek, however, is: "In beginning was the Word, and the Word was with the God, and
God was the Word." I have capitalized the word *Word* since
here it is clearly a title for Christ himself. This is seen later in
the same passage (v. 14) where it says, "and the Word
human being became and tented among us." The original
Greek does not distinguish between upper and lower case;
letters written in the "uncial" (that is, "inch-high") style
were all capitals. Hence the translators of the KJV and
other versions (including mine, above) that give *W*ord
instead of *w*ord are, admittedly, interpreting or "paraphrasing" at this point, trying to show what we think the
original author intended.

Further, the literal "in beginning" is not good English;
hence the word *the* has to be inserted before *beginning* to
make it read more smoothly. To this effort to translate
meaningfully and naturally—by using three English words
(in the beginning) for two Greek words (in beginning)—
there has evidently been no objection; even the most conservative, traditional translators are willing to let the *the*
stand. Dana and Mantey point out, however, that the ab-
sence of the article *the* in Greek here is not accidental since
"a prepositional phrase usually implies some idea of quality
or kind." That is in harmony with the basic evidence that
the lack of the article in Greek frequently emphasizes
quality rather than identity.[1]

In fact, there is no point that can be labeled "the beginning" as far as God is concerned; as limited creatures,
we have to think of time, of things starting and things
ending. From our point of view, whenever "the beginning"
occurred, the Word was already there, a fact further confirmed by the choice of the verb *was* (v. 1) in contrast to the
verb *became* (v. 14). The word *was* suggests a continuous
state of existence; in other words, "at the beginning"—if
it is possible to conceive of such a time—the Word already
"existed." It is this aspect of *being* that some of the more
dynamic-equivalent translations try to bring out. Thus,

"When the world began, the Word was already there" (WB); "When all things began, the Word already was" (NEB); "Before anything else existed, there was Christ" (LB); "In the beginning the Word existed" (CBW); and "Before the world was created, the Word already existed" (TEV).

Going back to our literal rendering of the Greek, we notice that the text says, "and the Word was with *the God,* and *God* was the Word." A further subtlety of the Greek language here is not brought out in the traditional rendering memorized by many of us. We learned to recite "with God" and "was God," as if the two occurrences of *God* in this verse were the same. As a matter of fact, they are not. The first one speaks of "the God," with the definite article in Greek because the personality of God is in focus. Christ's fellowship was "with God" identified as a person. The second *God* occurs without the article, which it may of course do because it is a proper name. It comes immediately after another reference to "the God" and not in the usual word order in Greek ("God was the Word"). *Word* is still clearly identified as "the Word," but the stress, accent or focus shifts in the final clause to the *character* of God rather than his personhood.

The Jehovah's Witnesses make much of the lack of the definite article with *God* here, as if this were clear proof that we must read "a god." Polytheism is not the point here at all, but rather the fact that the Word, who earlier was said to have existed "with" (actually, face to face with, in fellowship with) God, himself shared the character or nature of God. The verb *was* in all three clauses of verse 1 means "existed, continued in a state as."

Our English language does not lend itself to the same kind of subtlety found here in the Greek unless we expand it to a paraphrase—something like "At the beginning the Word existed, and the Word existed in fellowship with God; in fact [the *and* in Greek is often emphatic], the Word was himself Deity."[2] It is interesting to observe again how those translations that try to be more dynamic than formal have struggled with this verse and sought to bring out more of the underlying sense: "The Word dwelt with God, and what God was, the Word was" (NEB); "The Word was with God, and the nature of the Word was the same as the nature of God" (WB); " . . . Christ, with God. He has always been alive and is himself God" (LB); "and the Word was face to face with God; yea, the Word was God Himself" (CBW); "he was with God, and he was the same as God" (TEV).

I have gone into this verse in detail to show that *even our most traditional, formal-correspondence versions do not* (and, in fact, cannot) *render a verse such as John 1:1 without some paraphrasing,* adding or leaving out the article *the* changing the word order and so on.

As another example take the verb *chrēmatizō,* which means "to give a [divine or oracular] warning," the agent per se not being specified. In Luke 2:26 the agent is identified as "the Holy Spirit," in Acts 10:22 as "an angel" and in Hebrews 12:25 as (probably) Moses. In Matthew 2:12, 22 and Hebrews 8:5, although the agent is left unnamed in the Greek, the KJV and many other versions, including the TEV in Matthew 2:12 (but not v. 22) and Hebrews 8:5, specify that God did the warning.

Liberty Curtailed

To say that paraphrase is inevitable in translating is not to say that any paraphrase is legitimate. What principles can be laid down to guide translators of Holy Scripture in their work, especially when the distinction between translation and paraphrase becomes blurred?

Perhaps I can clarify the issue with a model often applied to synonyms to illustrate the similarity and the difference between two terms. Synonyms, incidentally, are "words which share several (but not all) essential components and thus can be used to substitute for one another in some (but not all) contexts."[3] The model is simply two ovals (one for each word being compared) which partially overlap:

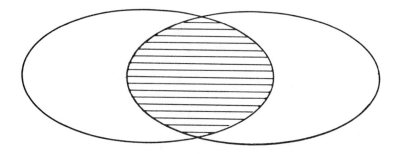

Such a model, expanded to allow for comparison of more than two synonyms (for example, *big, large, great*), might resemble a flower, with each petal (oval) standing for a word that overlaps the others to some degree. For our purposes, two ovals are sufficient, labeled thus:

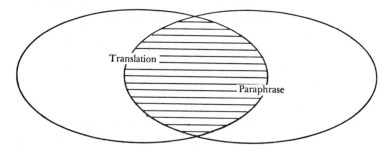

The two terms have some features in common (shown by the shaded area). Only in that overlapping area do translation and paraphrase become "synonymous." Outside that area the essential features of each term diverge.

Nida and Taber conclude their monumental work *The Theory and Practice of Translation* by calling attention to the question of how to judge a good translation. Their summary reminds us of the model we have been looking at above. In fact, we can superimpose the synonym model on Nida and Taber's summary by tracing the ovals (which they do not give) in over their model. The words are theirs; only the ovals and shaded area are mine.

What is a good translation? Perhaps we can answer this question by contrasting a good translation with bad translations of two kinds:

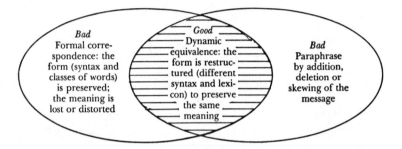

Bad Formal correspondence: the form (syntax and classes of words) is preserved; the meaning is lost or distorted

Good Dynamic equivalence: the form is restructured (different syntax and lexicon) to preserve the same meaning

Bad Paraphrase by addition, deletion or skewing of the message

On the one hand, it is possible to make a bad translation, as in column 1, by preserving the form at the expense of the content. On the other hand, it is possible to make a bad translation, as in column 3, by paraphrasing loosely and distorting the message to conform to alien cultural patterns. . . . This is the bad sense of the word "paraphrase." But, as in column 2, a good translation focuses on the meaning or content as such and aims to preserve that intact; and in the process it may quite radically restructure the form: this is paraphrase in the proper sense.[4]

It can be seen that both translation and paraphrase have good and bad aspects. When we use the word *translation* in a good sense (oval #1, shaded area; or column #2 in Nida and Taber's summary) we also necessarily include *paraphrase* in a good sense (oval #2, shaded area; or column #2 in the summary). It is not possible to do otherwise.

Certain principles or guidelines should help us to avoid either of the two bad extremes (the white part of ovals #1 and #2, or columns #1 and #3 of the summary). By concentrating on the common area, translation and paraphrase become essentially one. In these guidelines we will primarily be contrasting formal-correspondence translation and dynamic-equivalent translation—in other words, columns #1 and #2 of Nida and Taber's summary. The fact is that bad paraphrases (column #3) are neither as numerous as bad translations (column #1) nor as influential. The history of Bible translation provides us with far more examples of formal-correspondence renderings than of way-out paraphrases.

Five Guidelines

Avoid meaninglessness We translate/paraphrase in the good sense (that is, dynamically) when a literal/formal translation would be *meaningless*.

Amos 4:6 in many translations illustrates this principle. The KJV (followed by the RV, ASV, RSV, JB and NASB) in this verse says, "And I also have *given you cleanness of teeth* in all your cities, and want of bread in all your places: yet have ye not returned unto me, saith the LORD" (italics mine). The italicized words here represent "zero meaning"; they are not even likely to be taken in a wrong sense but simply ignored as obscure and conveying nothing in particular. Some dynamic-equivalent versions, however, make it clear that God had punished his people by sending them famine so that they had nothing to eat; hence, rather graphically, even their teeth were out of business. Since we do not talk that way in English, the TEV says, "I was the one who brought famine to all your cities, yet you did not come back to me." The LB has, " 'I sent you hunger,' says the Lord, 'but it did no good; you still would not return to me.' " The NEB tries to retain the imagery of teeth but with somewhat doubtful effect: "It was I who kept teeth idle in all your cities, who brought famine on all your settlements; yet you did not come back to me. This is the very word of the LORD."

In 1 Peter 1:13 (KJV), "gird up the loins of your mind" is meaningless in English today. The mind does not have "loins," and most people would not know how to "gird" them, or gird anything else, for that matter. More of the so-called modern translations should have clarified this to something like "have your minds ready for action" (TEV) or "prepare your minds for action" (NIV) rather than preserving the archaic rendering of 1611.

The average person would also have trouble making sense out of 2 Corinthians 6:12 (KJV), "Ye are not straitened in us, but ye are straitened in your own bowels." It is not that the word *bowels* is unknown to today's readers, only that they use it in an entirely different sense. The apostle Paul was not talking about some medical affliction but about an attitude, an affection missing in his readers. This is clearly brought out in the NIV, "We are not withholding our affection from you, but you are withholding yours from us," and in the TEV, "It is not we who have closed our hearts to you; it is you who have closed your hearts to us." Similarly, it is difficult to see any meaning in the word *bowels* in Philippians 2:1 (KJV), where "bowels and mercies" are joined together.

Finally, consider 1 Chronicles 26:18 in the following six versions:

"At Parbar westward, four at the causeway, and two at Parbar" (KJV).

"and for the parbar on the west there were four at the road and two at the parbar" (RSV).

"At the Parbar on the west there were four at the highway and two at the Parbar" (NASB).

"at the western colonnade there were four at the causeway and two at the colonnade itself" (NEB).

"Six guards were assigned each day to the west gate, four to the upper road, and two to the nearby areas" (LB).

"Near the western pavilion there were four guards by the road and two at the pavilion itself" (TEV).

A footnote in the RSV says that "the meaning of the word *parbar* is unknown," and a marginal note in the NASB observes that *parbar* means "possibly court or colonnade."

On such renderings with zero meaning, Nida and Taber point out that "to retain complete meaninglessness in the text is not satisfactory. It would be much better to attempt at least some of the plausible conjectures as to the meaning of *parbar* and to make sense of the passage. One could always caution the reader that the meaning of the verse is uncertain. But as a principle it is best at least to make sense in the text and put the scholarly caution in the margin, rather than to make nonsense in the text and offer the excuse in the margin."[5]

Avoid ambiguity We translate/paraphrase dynamically when a literal/formal translation would be *ambiguous*.

The Scriptures as we read them in translation are full of ambiguities, requiring many things (for example, persons, subjects, objects) to be supplied from the context. Individuals well taught in the Bible are often able to do this, but average readers cannot. They are as likely to draw the wrong conclusion as the right one.

For example, 1 Timothy 5:3 tells us to "honour widows that are *widows indeed*" (KJV, NASB), or " . . . who are real widows" (RSV). What is the meaning of "indeed" or "real" in these renderings? A widow is either a widow or she is not a widow, and adding "indeed" or prefixing "real" does not make it any clearer. The context (v. 5), however, does make it plain that a "widow indeed" is one who is "desolate" (KJV), who "has been left alone" (NASB). The ambiguity is therefore cleared up by such translations as the LB, "women whose husbands have died, if they don't have anyone else to help them," and TEV, "widows who really are all alone," or JBP, "widows who are really alone in the world."

Even the beloved twenty-third psalm in the traditional versions—"The LORD is my shepherd, I shall not want"—although comforting to hear because of its familiarity, is not English as it is used today. In current English *want* is no longer an intransitive verb meaning "to lack [something]" but a transitive one meaning "to desire [something]." People not conversant with Bible language might think that this verse means, "The LORD is my shepherd whom I will not want." The NEB preserves the verb *want* as transitive—"The LORD is my shepherd; I shall want nothing"—but this phrasing may be understood (in keeping with Buddhist doctrine) as a total lack of desire rather than an assurance that a person will *lack* nothing. Although we are not yet used to them, the renderings given in the LB ("Because the Lord is my Shepherd, I have everything I need!") and the TEV ("The LORD is my shepherd; I have everything I need") are much more accurate for twentieth-century readers.

Pronouns are often ambiguous in receptor languages. The English of Mark 1:9-10, for example, speaks of Jesus coming to be baptized by John. Then, immediately afterward, we are told that "he saw the heavens opened, and the Spirit like a dove descending upon him" (KJV). Who is the *he?* John (the immediate antecedent) or Jesus? The TEV and some other translations prefer the latter and make the reference specific. So, "As soon as Jesus came up out of the water, he saw heaven opening and the Spirit coming down on him like a dove."

As I and my colleagues were translating Mark 1:32 in the Urdu New Testament it was necessary to say that people brought *to Jesus* (not just "unto him," KJV) those who needed healing, since the most recent reference to a person was the *she* (Peter's mother-in-law) who "ministered to them" (v. 31). In Urdu the same word is used for he/she/it and for him/her/it—a fact that makes it extremely important to specify just who is performing a particular action. In the process of specifying, the most natural way of removing the ambiguity is to substitute a noun for the pronoun. That is why in Mark 1:45 we also had to say that people came "to Jesus," rather than to the man who was out broadcasting that he had been healed. Likewise in Mark 1:30 we were forced, in order to avoid ambiguity, to render "people told *Jesus* about her," using the name *Jesus* instead of the pronoun *him.* If we had used the pronoun in both places it could have meant either they told her about Jesus or they told Jesus about her.

In Judges 3:6 the KJV says, "And they took *their* daughters to be *their* wives, and gave *their* daughters to *their* sons, and served *their* gods" (italics mine). We have the word *their* five times in one verse, an ambiguity bound to produce confusion in any but the most determined reader. A similar ambiguity exists with the multiple uses of *he* and *him* in John 12:39-43, which should be cleared up in careful translation.

Occasionally a receptor language will require omission of a word repeated in the original in order to avoid ambiguity. For example, in the opening chapter of Luke's Gospel, Zechariah's "wife Elizabeth" is mentioned in verses 5 and 7. But to repeat the words in verse 13, "your wife Elizabeth," can—because in certain languages it is unnatural—convey the notion that Zechariah had another wife whose name was not Elizabeth, a situation which would not be at all strange in some cultures. In that case, either *wife* or *Elizabeth* is sufficient; but not both.

In Mark 6:16 (compare Lk. 9:9) we run across another kind of ambiguity where King Herod says, "It is John, whom I beheaded . . . " (KJV). We know from verse 27 that the king himself did not cut off John's head but "sent an executioner" to do it. Perhaps the verb *behead* in English can be construed as both active and causal; but in some languages one must use a form of the verb which shows that the king only had the deed done, or caused it to be done. In English, the TEV is accurate in saying: "He is John the Baptist! I had his head cut off, but he has come back to life!"

In contrast, on the other side of the causal issue, JBP says in Matthew 6:2, "Don't hire a trumpeter to go in front of you." The Greek merely says, "Sound no trumpet." Because there is no hint in the context that someone else is to do the trumpeting, to add the causal idea here is uncalled for. Lenski in fact, notes that "diligent search fails to verify the view that the Pharisees used trumpets to call the poor together and to assemble a crowd to witness their alms-giving. Nor would trumpets be used in a synagogue. This indicates that 'do not start trumpeting' is *figurative;* we should say, 'do not advertise.' "[6]

This principle does not require that every instance of ambiguity in Scripture be removed. Some ambiguity is obviously deliberate as, for example, Jesus' reference to "the leaven of the Pharisees and of the Sadducees" (Mt. 16:6); the confusion is not cleared up in the disciples' minds until verse 12. Rather, translators must be alert to the possibility of unintentionally introducing ambiguity. De Waard and Nida point out that

> most of what is obscure in the Scriptures is due to our ignorance of the historical and cultural backgrounds of the messages and not to the writer's intent to make the message unintelligible . . . and it is unfair to the original writer and to the receptors to reproduce as ambiguities all those passages which may be interpreted in more than one way.

> In the first place, the reader will almost inevitably acquire a wrong impression as to the intent or purpose of the biblical writer, since it will seem to the reader that the biblical writer was not concerned with communicating a message but only with "playing language games."

> In the second place, the translator places a very heavy burden on the receptor to determine which of two or more meanings may be involved, and the average reader is usually much less capable of making correct judgments about such alternative meanings than is the translator, who can make use of the best scholarly judgments on ambiguous passages.

> Accordingly, the translator should place in the text the best attested interpretation and provide in the marginal notes the appropriate alternatives.[7]

Avoid misleading translation We translate/paraphrase dynamically when a literal/formal translation would be *misleading.*

The highest priority in translation work must be given to intelligibility. Some have made such a fetish of "correctness" that they completely overlook the far deeper question of *correct for whom?* Thus Nida and Taber insist that "correctness must be determined by the extent to which the average reader for which a translation is intended will be likely to understand it correctly. Moreover, we are not concerned merely with the possibility of his understanding correctly, but with the overwhelming likelihood of it. In other words, we are not content merely to translate so that the average receptor is likely to understand the message; rather we aim to make certain that such a person is very unlikely to misunderstand it."[8]

Nida and Taber mention a specialist whose job it was to translate and interpret for the aviation industry. He commented that in his work he did not dare turn out the kind of rendering that Bible translators often do, on the grounds that "With us complete intelligibility is a matter of life and death."[9] All of us who travel by plane can be thankful that an aviation translator feels that way. But shouldn't we who regard the gospel message as a matter of life and death care deeply about the church not having a "feeling of urgency to make sense"?

Nida tells of a certain Polynesian who, when asked about a very literal translation of the Scriptures in his language, came out with a masterpiece of understatement, "It is a little bit clear."[10] Unfortunately, near the end of the second century of the modern missionary movement many people around the world have only some literal translation of the Bible—and still do not know what we are talking about.

Consider some examples of misleading translation. Eight times in the first two chapters of Amos we read the words, "for three transgressions . . . and for four" (KJV, RSV, NASB), all related to various cities and nations warned by the prophet of disaster coming upon them. The impression of readers is often one of surprise that God would punish people so severely for only three or four offenses. That interpretation is quite far from the facts. Although in Hebrew that temporal expression may refer to three or four literal occasions, it may also idiomatically be equivalent to saying "time after time" or "again and again." It seems obvious that Amos had in mind repeated or continual acts of wickedness. The formal-correspondence translations retain the literal (and thus misleading) form, while the more dynamically equivalent versions render it "again and again" (TEV, LB) or "for crime after crime" (NEB).

Two plus two equals four in mathematics, but not always in translation. That is to say, the whole is not always equal to the sum of its parts, as Romans 12:20 will illustrate. The famous words, "If thine enemy hunger, feed him; if he thirst, give him drink: for in so doing thou shalt heap coals of fire on his head" (KJV), are retained substantially the same in the RV, ASV, RSV, NASB, CBW, JB, NIV and, surprisingly, even in the LB, JBP and NEB. The idiom here, taken literally, is often understood at best to refer to what some call "Christian vengeance" and at worst to some perverse and novel way of torturing people to death. As a matter of fact, since it occurs in a passage that speaks against taking vengeance at all, it is obviously being misunderstood. What is meant is that by behaving in a "Christian way" the follower of Christ will make a person ashamed of his behavior. Only the TEV ("by doing this you will make him burn with shame") and WB ("if you do that, you will make him feel the pangs of burning shame") translate meaningfully and in a way not to be misunderstood.

Another translation likely to mislead may be seen in Luke 13:1 where we read about some Galileans "whose blood Pilate had mingled [mixed] with their sacrifices" (KJV, ASV, RSV, JB, NASB, NIV and even JBP and NEB). Some receptors into whose languages this has been translated have got the impression that Pilate was a sadist who took delight in stirring the meat of the Jewish animal sacrifices in the blood of the sacrificers whom he had killed. Whatever our image of Pilate may be, such a gross picture is not suggested by this verse. Rather, the sense is brought out by WB as "the Galilaeans whom Pilate had murdered at the very moment when they were offering their sacrifices," by the LB as "Pilate had butchered some Jews from Galilee as they were sacrificing at the Temple in Jerusalem" and by the TEV as "the Galileans whom Pilate had killed while they were offering sacrifices to God." Any of these dynamic renderings makes more sense than the traditional, literal one.

It is safe to say that the average twentieth-century reader does not have any idea what is meant by the expression "children of the bridechamber" (Mk. 2:19) and many other similar Semitic idioms found in our Bible. Rather than leaving them to misunderstand by reading something into the text that is not intended, the principles of translation encouraged in this book require that the words be translated as "friends of the bridegroom" (LB, WB, NEB), "wedding guests" (RSV, CBW, JBP, TEV, NIV) or some other similar phrase.

Romans 14:2 (RSV) says, "One believes he may eat anything, while the weak man eats only vegetables" (similarly rendered in the KJV and NASB). The word *weak* here (as also in 1 Cor. 8:9) has nothing to do with physical weakness caused by vegetarianism; it is weakness of faith (v. 1) that is meant. Consequently, a better translation of the verse gives "whose faith is weak" (NIV) or "who is weak in the faith" (TEV).

Revelation 3:20, where Jesus says he stands at the door and *knocks* can be grossly misunderstood in some cultures. Nida mentions one society where such an expression would imply that Jesus was a thief.[11] In that society thieves knock to see if anyone is inside; honest people would call, so that those inside the house could recognize their voice. To avoid misleading, it is necessary to have Jesus stand at the door and *call*.

Beekman and Callow cite a similar instance where a literal rendering in one West African language led to a meaning quite unintended by the translators. When Jesus asked James and John (Mk. 10:38) whether they could "drink the cup" that he was to drink, it was taken to mean that Jesus was challenging them to a drinking bout, to see who could down the most liquor.[12] Of the more recent translations to which I have been referring, only the TEV, LB and WB make any effort to show that the *cup* mentioned here refers to Jesus' impending sufferings.

The traditional rendering of Psalm 1:1 which speaks of the "blessed man" as one who, among other things, does "not stand in the way of sinners" can easily mislead the uninformed. Nowadays to stand in the way of something or someone means to prevent or hinder, to serve as an obstacle to that thing or person. What is meant here of course is "to associate with," a meaning brought out clearly only in the LB, "who do not hang around with sinners" (somewhat colloquial, but still making the point accurately).

Avoid complicated, heavy or obscure renderings We translate/paraphrase dynamically when a literal/formal translation would be *complicated, heavy* or *obscure.*

Although the examples I have given are largely from the English language, it should be remembered that many of the older crosscultural versions of the Bible followed essentially the revised versions in English (British of 1881 and 1885 and American of 1901). Therefore, to give examples from, say, the ASV (or similar versions) actually reflects what is found in many other languages around the world.

Take 2 Corinthians 3:10 as an example, given in the ASV as, "For verily that which hath been made glorious hath not been made glorious in this respect, by reason of the glory that surpasseth." Such ponderousness is hardly improved on by later revisions and translations. The words are English, to be sure, but the sentence structure is Greek; and the meaning is anyone's guess. To make sense of it today one has to turn to something like the NEB, "Indeed, the splendour that once was is now no splendour at all; it is outshone by a splendour greater still"; the TEV, "We may say that because of the far brighter glory now the glory that was so bright in the past is gone"; or the LB (an admitted paraphrase), "In fact, that first glory as it shone from Moses' face is worth nothing at all in comparison with the overwhelming glory of the new agreement."

Romans 5:15-16 contains abstruse wording in both the KJV and the ASV. The former reads, "But not as the offence, so also is the free gift. . . . And not as it was by one that sinned, so is the gift." It is next to impossible on the level of the surface structure here for any ordinary reader to make sense out of these words. Instead, one has to turn to more dynamic efforts at translation to find out what is going on. For example, "But the gift of God through Christ is a very different matter from the 'account rendered' through the sin of Adam. . . . Nor is the effect of God's gift the same as the effect of that one man's sin" (JBP). Or, "But God's act of grace is out of all proportion to Adam's wrongdoing. . . . And again, the gift of God is not to be compared in its effect with that one man's sin" (NEB).

We have seen the importance of adopting a structure in which the kernels (basic ideas) of a statement are clear and out in the open. Literal, word-for-word translations, even if shorter than dynamically equivalent ones, tend to be more difficult to understand for the simple reason that they preserve and perpetuate for us in English (or whatever receptor language we are dealing with) not the grammar and structure of English but of Hebrew, Aramaic and Greek. This is why such versions are more often praised as "faithful" than as "meaningful."

Many times the words that translators choose to employ mitigate against easy understanding. How often, for example, do you use *lugubriously* (Jas. 5:9 WB), *dénouement* (1 Tim. 6:15 JBP), *parricides/matricides* (1 Tim. 1:9 NEB), *conflagration* (Rev. 18:18 NEB), *pallet* (not even in the Greek, Jn. 5:12 NASB), *fowler* (Prov. 6:5 NASB), or even *furrows* (Jn. 12:24 LB)? Such a list does not take into account the archaic and pedantic vocabulary found in the KJV, ASV and even RSV. Those of us who have worked abroad in a crosscultural situation have seen translations of the Scriptures that are filled with high-sounding language seemingly designed not so much to communicate with ordinary people as to demonstrate the translator's learning.

When preparing common-language versions it is particularly important to avoid words that raise the level and add to the heaviness of the finished product. Usually this can be done by carefully restructuring the original in keeping with the demands of the receptor language. For example, when translating the reference to an "upper room" in Mark 14:15 in one language, we found that the word for "upper" was really on too high a level for the average reader, yet an improvised form, although intelligible and colloquial, seemed too low-class to use in the Scriptures. We solved the problem by rendering, "He will take you upstairs and show you a room." The room was thus obviously seen to be an upper one, but we did not have to call it that.

Idiomatic expressions—for example, "son of perdition" —must be put into common language if they are not to remain obscure. Perdition does not have "children" and such Semitic expressions have to be stated in a way that communicates. We do *not* translate *words;* we translate *meaning.* "Son of perdition" (referring to Judas, Jn. 17:12) means "one who is doomed to be lost" (CBW) or "the man who was bound to be lost" (TEV). The NIV's original "child of hell" and the LB's "son of hell" attempt to keep the Semitic flavor without actually communicating the meaning.

Many other expressions are too heavy in content to mean much literally in any language. Thus, "fruit of his loins" (Acts 2:30 KJV) becomes "his descendants." "To shut up one's bowels" (1 Jn. 3:17 KJV) has nothing to do with constipation (as one Mexican language group assumed),[13] but rather means "closes his heart against his brother" (TEV) or "has no pity on him" (NIV). And, "cool of the day" (Gen. 3:8 KJV, ASV, RSV, NASB) is literally "wind of the day," that is, the cool time of the day—namely, the evening.

A word of caution is in order when one is seeking simpler or better-known terms for some that may seem obscure to the average receptor. There are some religious terms or symbols—for example, *cross, sacrifice, lamb of God, shepherd*—which must be preserved. This is explained by de Waard and Nida: "Even though terms for such biblical symbols may involve a degree of obscurity, especially in a first translation, a close formal correspondence needs to be preserved for the sake of the integrity and unity of the biblical message. For example, people may not be acquainted with execution by crucifixion, but this does not justify the substitution of lynching, nor can one justify the use of 'little pig of God' for *lamb of God* merely because the people know little or nothing about sheep, but do highly prize their pigs."[14]

In many situations, however, no doctrinal or symbolic issue is at stake. For example, in one of the languages for which I have served as an adviser, a language belonging to a Hindu tribe, the translators raised the question of how to render Luke 15:23, 27, where the "fatted calf" (KJV; "prize calf," TEV) is mentioned. To Hindus nothing could be more reprehensible than killing a calf and then eating it. It is true that cattle are an important element in the Old Testament Levitical sacrificial system and at some point people will have to find this out. Yet the particular menu offered on this occasion when the prodigal son returned home is of no doctrinal consequence. The point is that his father put on the best meal he could to celebrate the occasion. In such a situation, where the offense would be so great as possibly to preclude any further reading of the Scriptures, it might be wiser to put into the text something like "he put on a great feast," or "he had the servants prepare the finest food they could," and then to indicate in a footnote that in those days people ate beef and to them the highest honor they could pay a guest was to offer him the meat of a prized calf, just as today in our tribe the best meal we could serve a guest would consist of _____ and _____.

Avoid unnaturalness Finally, we translate/paraphrase dynamically when a literal/formal translation would be *unnatural*.

This principle is another way of saying that each receptor language has certain obligatory features which must be observed. Some have already been pointed out.

Archaic terms in any language are certainly out of place in today's common-language versions of the Bible. In the old Urdu Bible, for example, when Jesus tells his disciples that men do not light a candle and put it under "a bushel" (Mt. 5:15 KJV), the word used for *bushel* (which even in English is outdated in this sense) is one which generations ago meant a measuring cup but today means a 12-inch ruler. How much sense does it make to tell people not to hide their light under a foot-ruler? Similar archaisms exist in the KJV—not surprising since it is now over 350 years old—although the preface to the NEB claims that the language of the King James Version was "already archaic when it was made," and is therefore even more so today.[15] Many of these archaisms, however, are so well known that I will not examine them here.

The old Urdu Bible (representative of many of the older formal-correspondence versions) has Jesus in John 15 call himself a "grape-*tree*" instead of a vine. There is a perfectly good word for *vine* in the language, and it is a mystery why the translators many years ago chose to coin their own term. The language used is not archaic but unnatural or artificial.

Earlier I discussed the question of connotative meaning. Also, when talking about common language, I referred to a level of language known as vulgar (which might include colloquialisms, slang and substandard grammar, as well as, occasionally, the really indecent). I noted that we could not put the Scriptures into language of that sort, and that even if the language per se was acceptable, we had to consider how it might *sound* to those who heard it—what it might suggest to them or conjure up in their minds.

Along this line, the word used in the old Urdu Bible for

"vain repetitions" in Matthew 6:7 is considered to be a low form of street language, for which far more suitable substitutes are available. Similarly, Jesus' rather peculiar reference in Mark 9:48 to "their worm" that "dieth not" and "the fire" that is "not quenched" (KJV, preserved even in some newer English translations) is translated just as literally into Urdu, but carries an obscene connotation so that those who hear it can scarcely repress a smile. Whatever it meant in the original, it was certainly not intended to make people laugh. As a matter of fact, CBW comes closer to bringing out the sense by saying "where the worm that feeds upon them never dies and the fire is never put out"; and JBP does even better, "where decay never stops and the fire never goes out." In the new Urdu translation we have given this as: "In hell [drawn from the context, vv. 43, 45, 47] people will go on rotting and the fire of that place will never stop burning."

Another instance of objectionable language in a "missionary" translation comes in the Urdu of Acts 19:16 (older rendering), where the wording is so risqué that it is difficult to read the passage aloud in the presence of a mixed audience.

The RSV, supposedly more modern than the KJV, claims to incorporate "simple, enduring words" and to be "intended for use in public and private worship."[16] So one wonders why it still preserves the rather crude rendering of the older versions in Matthew 24:19 and Luke 23:29 which speak of "those who give suck" and "breasts that never gave suck." What is simple and enduring about those words? Who uses such language today, even in private, let alone in public? The NASB only half bridges the euphemism gap by translating, "to those who nurse babes" (Mt. 24:19) and "the breasts that never nursed" (Lk. 23:29). Nowadays mothers don't have *babes;* they have babies. And what is wrong with considering *breasts* as a metonymy (a figure of speech where a part stands for the whole) for women?

Repetition of a word in English (and in Greek) often adds

emphasis. We say "very, very good," and Jesus says (in Jn. 3:
3, 5) "verily, verily" (KJV) or "truly, truly" (RSV, NASB).
But in some languages such repetition makes the expression weaker than if it were said only once.[17] Because of this
obligatory feature in those receptor languages and in order
for people to understand the message in a natural and
meaningful way, one of the *truly*s must be dropped.

In Matthew 2:18 a prophecy is quoted about Rachel
crying for her children because, as the Greek says, "they
are not." It is surprising that this stilted, unnatural form
of the KJV, RV and ASV is preserved in most modern versions today, which either give "they are not" or "they were
no more." Only the LB and TEV come out and say, as we
would in the twentieth century, that *they are dead.* If one's
friend, for example, died last year, one certainly does not
say, "I don't write to that friend anymore, because he is
not." Such English would sound ridiculous on our lips—yet
we put it between the covers of the Bible.

Another expression, common in both the Hebrew Old
Testament and the Greek New Testament, which when
translated into English and most other languages is unnatural and forced, is "to open the mouth and say or teach,"
as, "he opened his mouth, and taught them, saying, . . . "
(Mt. 5:2). In many languages the most natural way of expressing this idiom is simply to render, "He began to say" or
"He began to teach."

It is amazing how many unnatural and artificial expressions Bible readers are willing to put up with. Perhaps it
is because, as Knox pointed out, we have read them so often
in the Bible that we are not even aware of how strange and
foreign they sound to a person listening to the message for
the first time. I am not talking here about religious concepts
about which there might be some expected confusion; rather I refer to simple matters of everyday mundane grammar and usage. Leaving the KJV out of the debate entirely,
a reading of the parable of the prodigal son in Luke 15 of
the RSV (1946) and NASB (1971) shows how unnatural

renderings have become fixed in the language. Although many might be cited, a few examples are sufficient to illustrate the point.

Both versions (v. 12) speak of "the younger of them" while the NEB (1961) merely says "the younger." With comparatives involving only two persons the addition of "of them" is uncalled for.

The RSV (v. 13) says that the younger son "took his journey," an obsolete expression. We may "go on a journey" (as NASB) or "take *a* journey," or better yet "take a trip"; but nobody "takes *his* journey." The NEB simply says "left home."

The RSV (v. 15) says that he "joined himself," the NASB and NEB "attached himself," neither of which is as appropriate in modern English as "he went to work for" (TEV).

The RSV (v. 17) gives, "I perish here with hunger," a quite unnatural bit of translationese; the TEV's "here I am about to starve!" is at least an improvement. But a combination of the NEB's "here am I, starving to death!" with the TEV's rendering would be better still: "Here I am, starving to death!" This is how a person in that predicament probably would express himself today.

The RSV and the NASB (v. 22) speak of putting "a ring on his hand," a literal rendering of the Greek into pure translationese. We put bracelets on hands or arms, but we put rings only on fingers, noses and ears. The TEV, NEB, NIV, JBP and others give the correct and natural idiom for the English language.

The father in verse 24 says, "this my son" (RSV), not a natural manner of speaking today. The NIV, NASB and TEV say "this son of mine."

Although not all of the examples of unnatural renderings given in this section constitute an actual skewing (distortion) of the meaning of the original message, they nevertheless do represent a *stylistic* weakness. The warning given by de Waard and Nida is well taken:

one of the serious deficiencies of many Bible translations

is the inadequacy of the style. Readers may not be repulsed by the poor style, but at the same time they are not attracted to the message, since the words are selected and arranged in quite unsatisfactory ways. The ultimate acceptability of the translations seems to depend even more upon style than upon content. Apparently, people are much more concerned with the attractiveness of words than with the truth of the message. This does not mean that content should ever be sacrificed for the sake of style, but it does mean that the form of a message has a decisive influence upon its acceptance.[18]

Christian communicators, including Bible translators, must earn the right to be heard. They cannot automatically assume a ready-made audience, just waiting for them to "open their mouths" and teach them or "take up a pen" and translate for them. Translation of the Scriptures is more than just a philological activity—finding words in one language equivalent to words in another—as it is still considered by many to be. Translation is an act of communication involving the source language (or original text), the message (both its form and its meaning) and the receptors (or audience to be reached).

A people's language is one of their dearest possessions. They have rioted, revolted, seceded and even murdered for the sake of their mother tongue. If you don't think the issue is "sensitive," let someone criticize *your* speech, suggesting that it is incorrect, substandard or even pretentious, and see how you react. It is inappropriate to try to share the good news about Jesus Christ in language which, because it is inept and inadequate, communicates ineffectively or offensively—or not at all.

Even at best, and when preached by none other than an apostle Paul, the message about Christ's death on the cross (1 Cor. 1:18) was "nonsense" (TEV) to many, many people. It is not fitting for us who believe that message—to whom it is *not* nonsense—to add to its offense by presenting it in ambiguous, misleading, obscure, meaningless or unnatural terms—in other words, in jargon seemingly known only to the church and to God. People read each other's letters, their daily newspaper or the latest paperback in the language of daily life. Why should they not have God's Word available to them in a language they can understand and respond to?

CHAPTER 7

GOD'S WORD, BUT MAN'S LANGUAGE

I HAVE SUGGESTED that translation and paraphrase are two different aspects of the same process or, to use a figure of speech, they are two sides of the same coin. It would probably be more accurate to say that in their truest (that is, "good") sense they are not even two sides, but one and the same. They are of no more value separated than a coin split edgewise would be. The models on pages 97 and 98 show the reason why.

If the primary role of translators is to let authors speak for themselves in the receptor language, then paraphrase in the sense of "saying the same thing in other words" is inevitable.

I have shown that even the most staid and conservative translations of the Bible unwittingly include a considerable amount of paraphrase, though their supporters are reluctant to call it that.

Further, I have shown that the modern missionary movement with its emphasis on taking the Word of God "to every creature" has forced translators to take a new look at both their methods and results. Translators now recognize that obligatory features in a receptor language (English, as well as the lesser-known ones) arbitrarily determine many choices when one translates to bring out the content (dynamic equivalence) and not merely the form (formal correspondence). With form-oriented translation, concerned primarily with the source or original language, the receptors have to "make do" with the result as best they can. In contrast, content-oriented translation is primarily concerned with the meaning and impact of the message in the receptor language; with such translations the question of merely "making do" should not even arise.

I have indicated that although paraphrase is inevitable, it does have its bounds. The sky is not the limit, as some translators, reacting against the form-oriented method, may have forgotten. We translate/paraphrase/render Scripture "faithfully" only when we do not (either deliberately or unconsciously) add to, subtract from or distort the intent of the original author. Bible translation is not merely a "calling" but also a science and an art. Probably the quality most needed by translators—even more than ability, which I would not disparage in any way—is *humility*.

One of the greatest protections against exegetical errors is a profound respect for one's own ignorance, expressed in a firm determination not to introduce one's unique interpretations. Genuine humility is an essential ingredient in being a true "proxy source" and thus an important protection against the tendency to try to improve on the original, as when some translators try to harmonize the accounts of the descent of the Holy Spirit upon Jesus by changing the account in Mark 1.10 to agree with John 1.32, since they regard the Gospel of John as "more spiritual," hence more true. Some translators have even refused to render the statement "God repented himself," since they insist that God cannot change his mind, for he knows the end from the beginning. Apparently, it takes a special brand of intellectual honesty to let the Bible say things which seemingly contradict one's own theology.

Humility can also be a protection against showing off one's knowledge by introducing highly technical vocabulary or by insisting on literal translations as a means of revealing one's competence in Greek and Hebrew. Most of all, a spirit of humility combined with intellectual honesty can be the best insurance against the tendency to promote by means of Bible translating the cause of a particular theological viewpoint, whether deistic, rationalistic, [im]mersionist, millenarian, or charismatic.[1] Translators, whether individuals, groups, or committees, need to look inward as well as outward, and to be concerned not only with the message (back there) or the receptors (out there) but also with themselves (right here). The word is God's but the language is man's. Let translators beware, then, lest they fail to give both these factors their due.

NOTES

Chapter 1

[1]A. R. Bandini, "The Way of the Translator is Hard," *The Catholic World,* 167 (Apr. 1948), 60.

[2]Ronald Knox, *The Trials of a Translator* (New York: Sheed & Ward, 1949).

[3]Eugene A. Nida, "Translation or Paraphrase," *The Bible Translator* 1 (July 1950), 97.

[4]Robert Pick, "The Precarious Profession," *Saturday Review,* 33 (Sept. 30, 1950), 8.

[5]John Ciardi, "Translation—The Art of Failure," *Saturday Review,* 44 (Oct. 7, 1961), 17.

[6]John A. Kouwenhoven, "The Trouble with Translation," *Harper's Magazine,* 225 (Aug. 1962), 38.

[7]Robert Graves, "The Polite Lie," *The Atlantic,* 215 (June 1965), 74.

[8]Andrew R. MacAndrew, "The Hazardous Art of Mistranslation," *Harper's Magazine,* 232 (Apr. 1966), 94.

[9]Leo Rosten, "The Torments of Translation: Dismantling the Tower of Babel," *Harper's Magazine,* 245 (July 1972), 72-73.

[10]Reuben Brower, "Introduction: Translation as Parody," chapter 1 of *Mirror on Mirror* (Cambridge: Harvard Univ. Press, 1974).

[11]Gregory Rabassa, "If This Be Treason: Translation and Its Possibilities," *The American Scholar,* 44 (Winter 1974-75), 29.

[12]Ibid.

[13]Eugene A. Nida, *Language Structure and Translation*, essays selected and introduced by Anwar S. Dil (Stanford: Stanford Univ. Press, 1975), p. 24.

[14]Theodore Savory, *The Art of Translation* (London: Jonathan Cape, 1957), p. 103.

[15]Philip Schaff and Henry Wace, eds., *A Select Library of Nicene and Post-Nicene Fathers of the Christian Church*, second series, Vol. VI, *St. Jerome: Letters and Select Works* (Grand Rapids: Wm. B. Eerdmans Publishing Co., 1954) pp. 487b-488a.

[16]*Interpreter's Dictionary of the Bible*, ed. George Arthur Buttrick, vol. 4 (New York: Abingdon Press, 1962), p. 753a.

[17]Schaff and Wace, p. 44a.

[18]*The English Hexapla* (London: Samuel Bagster & Sons, 1841), p. 10.

[19]Flora Ross Amos, *Early Theories of Translation* (New York: Columbia Univ. Press, 1920), p. 62.

[20]*English Hexapla*, p. 43.

[21]Eugene A. Nida, *Toward a Science of Translating* (Leiden: E. J. Brill, 1964), p. 15.

[22]McCandlish Phillips, "Paraphrase of Scriptures Begets Success," *New York Times*, August 7, 1970.

[23]Eugene A. Nida, *Good News for Everyone: How to Use the Good News Bible (Today's English Version)* (Waco: Word Books, 1977), p. 9.

[24]Mark Van Doren, "The Uses of Translation," *The Nation*, 170 (May 20, 1950), 474.

[25]Gerald F. Hawthorne, "How to Choose a Bible," *Christianity Today*, December 5, 1975, p. 10.

[26]Kouwenhoven, p. 38.

[27]Ibid., p. 40.

[28]Nida, *Toward a Science of Translating*, p. 20.

[29]Eugene A. Nida, "Issues and Insights in Bible Translating," *Theology, News and Notes* (Mar. 1977), p. 5.

[30]Ibid., p. 19.

[31]Elsa Gress, "The Art of Translating," in *The World of Translation*, papers delivered at the Conference on Literary Translation, New York City, May 1970 (New York: P. E. N. American Center, 1971), p. 55.

[32]Pick, p. 41.

[33]Bandini, p. 61.

[34]Ibid.

[35]Ibid., p. 60.

[36]Nida, "Translation or Paraphrase," p. 97.

[37]See Sakae Kubo and Walter Specht, "Appendix," in *So Many Versions? Twentieth Century English Versions of the Bible* (Grand Rapids: Zondervan Publishing House, 1975).

[38]John Beekman and John Callow, *Translating the Word of God* (Grand Rapids: Zondervan Publishing House, 1974), pp. 20-21.

[39]Nida, *Toward a Science of Translating*, p. 22.

[40]Ibid., p. 27.

[41]Nida, "Translation or Paraphrase," p. 105.

Chapter 2

[1]*Oxford English Dictionary,* compact edition in 2 vols., II (Oxford: Clarendon Press, 1971), p. 3381d.

[2]Ibid.

[3]Ibid., I, p. 1467c.

[4]Ibid., II, p. 2075b.

[5]Ibid.

[6]Beekman and Callow, p. 21.

[7]Ibid., italics mine.

[8]Eugene A. Nida and Charles R. Taber, *The Theory and Practice of Translation* (Leiden: E. J. Brill for the United Bible Societies, 1969), p. 47.

[9]Barclay Newman, Jr., "The Old Way and the New Way," *The Bible Translator,* 28 (Apr. 1977), 206-7.

[10]Nida and Taber, p. 39.

[11]Nida, "Translation or Paraphrase," pp. 105-6, italics mine.

[12]Eugene A. Nida, *Customs & Cultures: Anthropology for Christian Missions* (New York: Harper & Brothers, 1954), p. 296, italics mine.

[13]F. F. Bruce, *The English Bible* (New York: Oxford Univ. Press, 1970), p. 223.

[14]Ibid.

[15]Robert G. Bratcher, "The Living New Testament Paraphrased," book review in *The Bible Translator,* 20 (July 1969), 39, 131.

[16]Knox, pp. 14-15.

[17]Schaff and Wace, p. 113b.

[18]Eugene A. Nida, "Bible Translation in Today's World," *The Bible Translator,* 17 (Apr. 1966), 60.

[19]Nida, *Toward a Science of Translating,* pp. 15-16.

[20]Ibid., p. 18.

[21]Ibid.

[22]Nida, *Language Structure and Translation,* pp. 265-66.

[23]Ibid., p. 190, italics mine.

Chapter 3

[1]Frederick C. Grant and H. H. Rowley, revisers, Hastings' *Dictionary of the Bible,* 2nd ed., rev. (Edinburgh: T. & T. Clark, 1963), p. 348b.

[2]William F. Arndt and F. Wilbur Gingrich, *A Greek-English Lexicon of the New Testament and Other Early Christian Literature* (Chicago: Univ. of Chicago Press, 1957), p. 148a.

[3]Ibid., p. 475b.

[4]Schaff and Wace, p. 117b, italics mine.

[5]Ibid., p. 113b.

[6]Compare Kubo and Specht, p. 26.

[7]H. E. Dana and Julius R. Mantey, *A Manual Grammar of the Greek New Testament* (New York: The Macmillan Co., 1943), pp. 137-40.

Chapter 4

[1]Newman, p. 201.

[2]Nida, *Toward a Science of Translating,* p. 21.

[3]Howard G. Hendricks, *Say It With Love* (Wheaton, Ill.: Victor Books/SP, 1975), pp. 32-33.

[4]Kubo and Specht, p. 22.

[5]Ibid.

[6]*Twentieth Century New Testament: A Translation into Modern English*, rev. ed. (New York: Fleming H. Revell Co., 1904), p. iii.

[7]Knox, p. 9.

[8]Ibid., p. 8.

[9]Ibid., pp. 8-9.

[10]Nida, *Language Structure and Translation*, pp. 79-80.

[11]Adolf Deissmann, *The New Testament in the Light of Modern Research* (London: Hodder & Stoughton, n.d.), p. 76. The Haskell Lectures given at Oberlin College, Ohio, 1929.

[12]Adolf Deissmann, *Philology of the Greek Bible* (London: Hodder & Stoughton, 1908), p. 42.

[13]Hermann Cremer, *Biblico-Theological Lexicon of New Testament Greek* (Edinburgh: T. & T. Clark, 1880), p. iv.

[14]Ibid.

[15]Joseph Henry Thayer, *A Greek-English Lexicon of the New Testament* (Edinburgh: T. & T. Clark, 1930), pp. 693-96.

[16]Ibid., p. 688.

[17]James Hope Moulton and George Milligan, *The Vocabulary of the Greek New Testament (illustrated from the papyri and other non-literary sources)* (London: Hodder & Stoughton, 1930), pp. xii-xiii.

[18]James Hope Moulton, *A Grammar of New Testament Greek*, Vol. 1, Prolegomena (Edinburgh: T. & T. Clark, 1949), p. 242.

[19]James Hope Moulton, *From Egyptian Rubbish Heaps* (London: Kelly, 1916), p. 12.

[20]Compare Deissmann, *The New Testament in the Light of Modern Research*, p. 80.

[21]Adolf Deissmann, *Light from the Ancient East* (New York: Harper & Brothers, 1922), pp. 71-72.

[22]Cited by A. T. Robertson, *A Grammar of the Greek New Testament in the Light of Historical Research* (New York: Doran [Hodder & Stoughton], 1915), p. x.

[23]Deissmann, *Light from the Ancient East*, p. 78.

[24]Ibid., p. 81.

[25]Ibid., p. 82.

[26]Ibid., pp. 82-83.

[27]Camden N. Cobern, *The New Archaeological Discoveries (and their bearing upon the New Testament and upon the life and times of the primitive church)* (New York: Funk and Wagnalls, 1928), p. 31.

[28]Nida, *Language Structure and Translation*, p. 33, italics mine.

[29]Beekman and Callow, pp. 33-34.

[30]Norman Mundhenk, "What Translation Are You Using?" *The Bible Translator*, 25 (Oct. 1974), 419-20.

[31]Nida, *Language Structure and Translation*, p. 97.

[32]Newman, p. 206, italics mine.

[33]Kubo and Specht, p. 143.

[34]Nida, *Toward a Science of Translating,* p. 192.

Chapter 5

[1]Amos, p. 59.

[2]Nida, *Toward a Science of Translating,* p. 17.

[3]Ibid., p. 20.

[4]Savory, p. 24.

[5]Nida, *Toward a Science of Translating,* p. 21, italics mine.

[6]Clarence W. Hall, "Two Thousand Tongues to Go," condensed book section in *Reader's Digest,* 73 (Aug. 1958), 197.

[7]Ibid., p. 198.

[8]Everett C. Parker, "Scripture and the Machine," *The Christian Century,* 78 (Mar. 15, 1961), 327, italics mine.

[9]Ibid., p. 328.

[10]Eugene A. Nida, *God's Word in Man's Language* (New York: Harper & Brothers, 1952).

[11]Nida, *Toward a Science of Translating,* pp. 25-26.

[12]Graves, p. 80.

[13]Norman Mundhenk, "The Subjectivity of Anachronism," essay in Matthew Black and William A. Smalley, eds., *On Language, Culture, and Religion: In Honor of Eugene A. Nida* (The Hague/Paris: Mouton, 1974), p. 262.

[14]Nida, *Toward a Science of Translating,* p. 159.

[15]Nida and Taber, p. 4.

[16]Arndt and Gingrich, p. 682a.

[17]Nida and Taber, pp. 163-64.

[18]Compare William L. Wonderly, *Bible Translations for Popular Use* (London: United Bible Societies, 1968), pp. 149-51.

[19]Nida and Taber, p. 39.

[20]Ibid., pp. 33-35.

[21]Nida, *Customs & Cultures,* pp. 16-17.

[22]Ibid., p. 206.

[23]J. B. Phillips, *The New Testament in Modern English,* rev. ed. 1972 (London: Collins, 1973), pp. ix-x.

Chapter 6

[1]Dana and Mantey, p. 150.

[2]Compare ibid., pp. 140, 150, 251.

[3]Nida and Taber, p. 73.

[4]Ibid., p. 173.

[5]Ibid., p. 30.

[6]R. C. H. Lenski, *The Interpretation of St. Matthew's Gospel* (Minneapolis: Augsburg Publishing House, 1943), pp. 256-57, italics mine.

[7]Jan de Waard and Eugene A. Nida, *Bible Translating,* chapter 1 of unpublished book (Xeroxed), pp. 2, 22-23.

[8]Nida and Taber, p. 1.

[9]Ibid.

[10]Nida, *Customs & Cultures,* p. 217.

[11]Ibid., p. 218.

[12]Beekman and Callow, pp. 23-24.

[13]Nida, *Customs & Cultures,* p. 217.

[14]De Waard and Nida, p. 22.

[15]*New English Bible* (London: Oxford/Cambridge Univ. Press, 1972), p. v.

[16]*Revised Standard Version: The New Oxford Annotated Bible with the Apocrypha,* ed. Herbert G. May and Bruce M. Metzger (New York: Oxford Univ. Press, 1977), pp. xvi, xii.

[17]Compare Nida, *Customs & Cultures,* p. 206.

[18]De Waard and Nida, p. 13.

Chapter 7

[1]De Waard and Nida, p. 15.

Subject Index

Scripture Index